Discover Yourself On The Yellow Brick Road

Discover Yourself On The Yellow Brick Road

7 Core Principles of Career Success

Wendy Dashwood-Quick

First Published in Great Britain 2009 by www.BookShaker.com

Typeset in Book Antiqua

Dedication

There are numerous people I would like to take a moment to thank, whose influence on my life and thinking has been significant. I am taking this opportunity to pass on my appreciation to those great teachers in the field of Personal Development who set me on this path. Since commencing this project I have been amazed at the people I've connected with and the coincidences that have taken place to guide me to its completion.

I gratefully acknowledge the encouraging words given to me by friends and associates which helped me begin this project, including my Coach Allison Marlowe, Tom Evans, Gail Smirthwaite, Mike and Julie Gingel, Pavlenka Small, Paul McKie and Jan Marchant. During the past five years since becoming a coach, I have forged some super friendships, and have had the pleasure and privilege of meeting some incredible people.

I give heartfelt gratitude to my mother who is arguably my biggest fan, and my four amazing sisters Jules, Dee, Liz and Penny who always keep my feet on the ground, and always make me laugh. I really don't know what I'd do without them. I'd especially like to thank my friends who are always so enthusiastic and encouraging about my work. I am deeply indebted to my clients, for without them this book wouldn't even exist, and masses of thanks go to Debbie Jenkins of Lean Marketing who has left no stone unturned in helping me create my own little masterpiece.

Lastly, I would like to give a mention to The Business Café, Ecademy and those professionals and small business owners who keep the wheels of commerce going every day in their own way and from whom I have learnt so much.

SPECIAL ACKNOWLEDGEMENTS

Christine McPherson – Copy Editor
mcpherson.christine@googlemail.com

A massive vote of thanks go to Christine for her tireless editing and proof reading of this curious book full of stories, exercises and case studies. The second pair of eyes and her insights has been invaluable in helping me to keep going, as this project did eventually turn into a mammoth undertaking.

For my Dad, Peter - the inspiration behind my work and the reason I became a Coach.

Praise For This Book

"What a fantastic, straightforward and honest book, brimming with tools tips and tactics. It is rare to find such honest advice in such an accessible format. Anyone who's looking for some solid Personal Development strategies to become more effective, then look no further."

Jonathan Jay
Founder and Managing Director of SuccessTrack,
Author of 'Sack Your Boss'

"...I took your book to the beach today. It is the first time I have ever read a book cover to cover in one sitting, didn't move until I'd finished. I am now sunburnt down one side."

Kevin Nolan
Stockbroker & Financial Adviser, Edward Jones

Foreword

What a delightful book this is. I think people will love it. Wendy's writing is well-organised, perceptive, honest, funny, imaginative, and nourishing.

I love the way she weaves in the Wizard of Oz story as a rich source of archetypal common sense with salient quotes and story characters linked to people who face challenges and make positive changes. Wendy becomes your coach by giving you activities to do on your own 'Yellow Brick Road'. She creates a bright rainbow of seven principles for making your personal and professional dreams come true.

Wendy shines light on human fundamentals such as beliefs and intuition. She talks about emotions, the warning lights we can't ignore. She's spot on saying soft skills are essential for surviving in these times of change. She spotlights NLP, EFT and other soft skills and gives sound advice on public speaking, listening and communication. Who better to teach body language than someone who knows Flamenco dancing!

Wendy ranges widely, for example sharing personal stories and highlighting the importance of eating properly and coaching that creates positive change in the world – so how could I not be an enthusiastic fan?

There are good new questions for your repertoire. As a question 'affectionado' I relish Wendy's 'Power Questions', especially the attitude question – who wouldn't?

The seven core principles could, in Wendy's words, help you devise an orchestrated plan. You'll have tangible results - soon.

I'll be thumbing my copy time and again for helpful images, focus and friendly nudges into action.

Judy Barber
Author of Good Question! The Art of Asking Questions
To Bring About Positive Change, www.judybarber.net

Contents

Preface

Are you contemplating a career change or aspire to be personally and professionally more effective? In the 21st century employers value high quality staff who possess more than just a good degree and an impressive CV. In a nutshell, it's not so much what you know, but who you are that matters, and unlike 20 years ago when you could walk out of one job on Monday and start a new one by Tuesday, the job market is very competitive, and employers can be more choosy. Therefore, Self Development is now coming into its own. The best leaders, the best managers, the best salesmen and women are those who take the time to develop themselves.

But how can you get to the front of the queue, or successfully lead or influence others if you are 'in your own way', meaning you're stressed, overwhelmed, uninspired in your role, facing change or confused by too much choice. Would you like to be more influential and able to handle everything that's being thrown at you right now?

What follows are 7 Core Principles brought together as a coaching system. This very straightforward system will enable you to develop yourself literally from the ground up. You can start here, from scratch by incorporating a ton of knowledge and expertise that I have crammed into 300 odd pages. These principles, based around the work of Robert Dilts, NLP plus my work with my coaching clients, are presented in a user friendly way and are easy to understand and implement.

This personal enhancement programme is a targeted, cohesive process and will apply if you are currently employed or changing directions altogether. We live in a tough world which dictates that we adopt strategies to become mentally, physically and emotionally tougher in order to thrive.

I am sharing these principles and all my expertise with you because I believe we need to go back to basics and work with stronger more meaningful values. Over the past few decades our principles have been eroded and replaced with flimsy values which have led to a general lowering of standards. We've been lured away from the path with the promise of instant results whilst forgetting that lasting achievement entails sacrifice, dedication and commitment to excellence.

You are where you are today as a result of the conscious choices and decisions you've made up until this point. Therefore I hope that these principles will influence the quality of the decisions you make and produce more successful and satisfying results in your life and work.

WHY DID I WRITE THIS BOOK?

I heard a great quote the other day: "The person with experience will always triumph over the person with a theory." So here I am, a real person who's helped real people, with real issues, talking to you – a real person. But that's only half the story.

Firstly, my family background meant that I have been destined to fulfil this role as a coach. I've been 'thrown in at the deep end' so many times it made sense to share my knowledge and help other people.

A series of bizarre reversals of fortune have been a feature of my life, and I was curious to understand why and what I am destined to become. Eventually I came across the field of Personal Development which has helped me develop and grow as a person. I'd rather read a book on personal growth than a novel.

In my career as a PA I'd hit the glass ceiling and begun to question where I was really going. I had already outgrown the role by the time I underwent my coaching training. A good PA is skilled at multi-tasking, an excellent diplomat, discreet, and well organised; they possess a massive arsenal of skills. Over the last 25 years I've worked for dozens of Executives at all levels giving me a unique insight into human nature. However, I realised my career wasn't going anywhere, despite all the work I had done to develop myself and my skills. I knew that I needed something else, and new vistas to explore which were much more meaningful for me.

Then in 2003 I was made redundant; I didn't immediately know what to do next as I'd been in a safe, cosy cocoon for the previous 13 years.

Coincidentally, during those 13 years I'd developed an interest in sports coaching. Each summer the company that I worked for held a rounders tournament and every year I coached a team that consistently did really well. This convinced me that I had a bit of a gift. Once a year I would turn a motley crew of people (some of whom had virtually no hand-eye coordination at all, or had never even heard of rounders) into a winning squad. They always came through for me on the day.

I used a 'method' that the competition couldn't quite fathom (and to be honest even I wasn't sure what it was). Each summer before the tournament, other teams would send 'spies' to find out what our strategy was, or they'd try and 'headhunt' me to captain their side. They'd ask me "what's your secret?" That got me thinking.

Looking at the bigger picture; the celebrity culture, consumerism, the media and the instant gratification society has driven down our principles and values. We need to be held individually accountable and make a greater contribution to society, and not become voyeuristic spectators, standing by whilst everything around us begins to deteriorate. Many people are looking around them and beginning to ask questions. They realise they also need to take greater interest in the future of planet Earth, and must view it less as a resource to be plundered, but something to be nurtured and appreciated.

At an individual grass roots level, I feel it is essential for each of us to take the time to develop, understand and take responsibility for our own wellbeing, and the consequences of our choices and actions.

"We live in a highly materialistic society. By 'materialistic' here we mean a value set which believes that material goods will lead to well-being to the exclusion of focusing on other factors. The evidence shows, however, that materialistic people are less happy. Material consumption is also the primary driver of many of our environmental problems. It is obviously extremely difficult for policy to intervene to change cultural norms."
Source: NEF (New Economic Foundation)

However, what this book aims to deliver is a long-term strategy, which requires commitment on the part of you, the reader. This is where Coaching comes in.

Let me say now coaching isn't about designer handbags! If anything has the potential to change the world and transform anyone's life, career or business, coaching is it because it connects you with your highest and best self and away from material concerns. Let's face it, when you finally leave this earth, you're very unlikely to be thinking "I wish I'd bought a bigger flat screen TV or more shoes" are you?

WHY 7 PRINCIPLES?

So, down to business. How exactly do you develop yourself and 'get out of your own way'?

Over the years I started to see familiar patterns of thinking and behaviour with some of my clients. It seemed that whenever they weren't moving forward or were stuck or confused, I found it easier to explain why by drawing a simple diagram. The logical levels diagram created by Robert Dilts.

Time and time again I would be drawn to this diagram. It has been so useful in helping my clients see where they were on their journey, and what they needed to change to reach their objectives.

As you read this book (and not every chapter will apply to you of course), if any aspect of your career (or life) isn't working out, you may find some answers here.

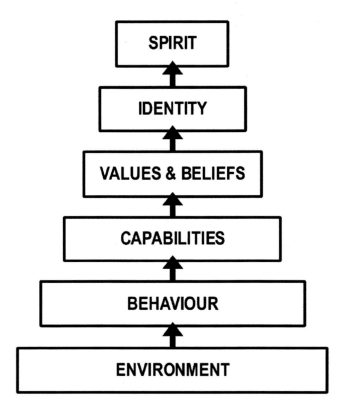

As you can see the key words of this process are depicted in a pyramid, and represent our journey as we prepare to self-actualise. By progressing through these levels you can confront any interference you may encounter, which might be stopping you from reaching your objectives. You will thus gain clarity, and a greater degree of certainty about who you are, what you want and where you're going, and for some clients who've already been through this process, - it is a totally liberating experience.

In our routine day-to-day lives it's almost impossible to attain this level of clarity because we rarely give ourselves the space to pause, think and reflect. We need to be like a painter and step back periodically to review our progress and get 'the bigger picture' of our life.

WHAT CAN THIS BOOK DO FOR YOU?

Through this book I will become your personal coach. A coach acts as a facilitator and an objective observer. The resultant energy produced between the coach and the client, creates a "third mind" which brings forth intangible benefits e.g. ideas, solutions and breakthroughs. It is the intangible stuff that you cannot measure, which produces outcomes which are invariably priceless in their significance.

Use this book to learn how to 'get out of your own way' and clarify your objectives. Then the door will open to usher in new and significant changes in your life and work.

"The first fundamental law of the Universe is the law of three forces, or three principles, or, as it is often called, the law of three. According to this law, every action, every phenomenon in all worlds without exception, is the result of a simultaneous action of three forces – the positive, the negative and the neutralising. There is a super being in all of us. It is just a matter of working hard to find him."
Andrew Laurance, "The Other You"

7

Here are some examples of the specific results that have been achieved through coaching…

- The undergraduates who got to grips with their studies and passed their exams.
- The graduate who grabbed the opportunity of a lifetime to work abroad.
- The housewife who took the first steps to developing a business idea.
- The senior manager who repaired the strained relationships with her children.
- The manager who got a life instead of becoming a burnt-out workaholic.
- The woman who found the confidence to accept a dream job offer.
- The small business owner who got to grips with his time management.
- The entrepreneur who got his wife to stop nagging and start supporting him instead.
- The student who stopped loathing and started loving herself.
- The executive who was lost in the detail but then prioritised and took control.
- The businesswoman who started to value herself and her time thus reducing her stress levels.
- The administrator who bounced back after repeated failure and rediscovered her self confidence.
- The executive who found a new direction after retirement.
- The families of all these people who've all breathed a sigh of relief!

Wendy Dashwood Quick

The Path To The Yellow Brick Road

"Dorothy lay down at once, with Toto beside her soon fell into a sound sleep. The Scarecrow, who was never tired, stood up in another corner and waited patiently until morning came."
The Wonderful Wizard of Oz, L. Frank Baum

Dan 'Scarecrow' Burnside sat facing the locum at the Doctor's Surgery. His usual GP was absent today, but the man sitting before him looked strangely familiar, in fact he was probably the happiest and jolliest Doctor he'd ever met in his life. He read the nameplate on the desk which read 'Dr. M. Unchkin'. He was so short Dan could barely see him over the desk, as the Doctor read out the roll-call of stress related ailments that Dan was suffering with – Irritable Bowel Syndrome, High Blood Pressure, High Cholesterol and he had recently added eczema and a stomach ulcer to the list. Dan was constantly hyped-up and 'wired'. Paradoxically however, he was very successful and actually thrived on stress until very recently. Because success came at a price. The trouble was there were only 24 hours in a day and he was constantly running around like a headless chicken. Dan worked extremely hard but he regularly missed meals, rarely took any time off and frequently over committed himself.

This was beginning to affect his health, his behaviour and his relationships. In fact, he had started to realise that if he didn't stop and take stock, he would burn out altogether and his marriage would be in ruins. Dan was literally coming apart at the seams. His chaotic lifestyle was reflected in his out of control blond hair and appearance, even though he only wore the most expensive suits and bought ludicrously expensive shoes.

The Doctor continued, "Now, Mr Burnside, I've looked at your notes and it's becoming increasingly evident that it's a lifestyle thing. You need to get a grip on your stress levels, because I'm not going to prescribe any more drugs. To be honest with you, they wouldn't do you any favours anyway. "

"Oh," thought Dan. "So what are you going to do for me instead?" he asked.

The locum stood up and walked around the desk. He really was so short that even standing up he wasn't any taller;

just incredibly rotund. He paused, "No Dan – it's not what I'm going to do for you, it's what you are going to do for yourself. You need 'The 7 Core Principles'.

"What are The 7 Core Principles?" asked Dan.

"They are 7 Principles for a successful life. It's a programme that I introduce to hopeless cases like you to."

"Flaming nerve!" thought Dan viciously as he stared at the Doctors very large belly.

"You need a complete overhaul of your time management, work life balance and personal priorities before it's too late. I don't want to see you back here in a few months time, when you're about to have a heart attack."

- Dan had to admit that he struggled with his time management.

- He found it hard to delegate, ask for help and say no to anyone's demands.

- He enjoyed taking on the whole world with one hand tied behind his back, and still be home in time for tea!

His success was reflected in the car, the bank account and the big house. However, he knew that he must learn to use his head to work out a new strategy otherwise he could lose everything, but there wasn't enough time to stop and think these days!

The Doctor gave Dan a copy of an old battered book with instructions to read it in the next week and then return the book. Dan thanked the Doctor and took the book. It started to snow as he walked into a new pub restaurant that had just opened in the town and ordered a drink. He stared into the flames of a newly lit fire for about five minutes. He felt punch drunk. Then he sent an e-mail to his PA via his Blackberry, "Hi Glinda, I'm having problems with the Merc. May be some time. Cancel all my appointments." He found a seat tucked away in the corner, opened the book and started to read. He found the book so enticing, he couldn't put it down. It was the first book he'd read in years.

Louisa Lyons sat on the tube as she recalled yesterday's phone conversation with her best friend on her way home. There were no trains from Fenchurch St Station tonight so she had to take the District Line from Tower Hill tube station instead. "… and then because I got a bit upset about my handbag being stolen at lunchtime, my boss locked me in my office and told me to calm down. Then she went off to fetch the Chief Admin Officer, saying it was now a disciplinary matter because I was being hysterical. Nobody in the office likes her. They call her the Wicked Witch of the West."

Her friend sighed heavily as she listened to the litany of disasters that was the life of Louisa. Her friend finally interrupted, "Louisa you need to record everything that might happen from now on because it sounds very ominous. You need to protect yourself. This wicked witch of the west character sounds a real threat, and it doesn't sound as if she'll be flying away on her broomstick any time soon. In the meantime it's time you learned about the 7 Core Principles."

"What's that?" asked Louisa.

"It's 7 Core principles for a successful life. Why don't you buy a copy tomorrow, you can read it on the train every evening on your way home," replied her friend.

Louisa admitted to herself that her confidence had taken a bit of a nose-dive. She:

- Realised she needed to change something in order to get a promotion or at least move on.

- Doubted her ability to succeed.

- Felt a failure with each encounter with her boss. Her courage and motivation was ebbing away.

She was also paralysed with inertia and very indecisive these days. Louisa was beginning to wonder whether she would ever be recommended for a promotion, even though she was intelligent and had a first class honours degree. She couldn't work out why she wasn't being taken seriously. The great paradox of her life was that although she was a sissy at work, she was a keen hockey player and as brave as a blizzard on the hockey pitch. She cut a very striking figure with her mass of blond curly hair fearlessly charging towards her opponents. In that situation it really was a case of "yeah bring it on".

Tom Tindall-Heart sat on the fast train to Norwich at Platform 18 at Liverpool Street Station. He thought about the pretty girl he'd talked to last night on the train on his way home from a night out. He'd spent the entire journey telling her about how he hated his job in reinsurance and despised his bosses. He didn't have the motivation to resign because he was so far into his comfort zone the thought of doing something different was frankly really scary. However, there were hints of redundancies in the air, and that was even scarier! But he had to admit that his heart just wasn't in his job any more.

Here he was, sat staring at the book the girl had given him as she left the train. He gazed at the front of the book. She said she had no need for it now, and happily passed it onto him. He knew that if he was honest his career lacked passion, challenge and inspiration. He:

- Would dearly love to get out of the rat race and try something new, but he had no idea how or where to start. Although he loved garden design, working with wood and the great outdoors.

- Was beginning to doubt whether a satisfying career actually existed.

- Felt resentful and jealous of other people who all appeared to have more rewarding and fulfilling careers – sometimes he even resented the smiling postman who he bumped into once in a blue moon.

He was firmly wedged in a rut but was aware he might wake up one day to the realisation that life and technology had passed him by. Everyone else was talking about strange websites like Facebook, Twitter and 'blogging'. He couldn't get his head around the whole technology thing.

He was beginning to think he was having a mid-life crisis, because the only thing that remotely interested him at the moment was making sure that he looked well turned out for the office. Tom looked immaculate in his slate-grey suit, black shirt and silver tie which perfectly coordinated his jet-black hair and mesmerising coal black eyes.

"Read it tonight", the girl said as she slipped off the train. He reflected on this as he watched her walk away along the platform, in her perfectly small, sparkly red shoes…

"Goodbye, Tinman. Oh, don't cry! You'll rust so dreadfully. Here's your oil can."
Dorothy, The Wizard of Oz

WHAT'S GETTING IN THE WAY OF YOUR SUCCESS?

Let's be honest, invariably the core component that's preventing some of us from succeeding invariably boils down to the same thing… ourselves.

We manifest little annoying gremlins which influence our thoughts, our attitude, affecting our motivation and behaviour.

Ultimately your performance at work will suffer.

The technical term for gremlins is interference and it's interference that 'gets in our way'.

I am good friends with an Image/Branding consultant and her philosophy is this: "When you stand up in front of an audience and feel great in your clothes and aren't obsessing about what you look like, you get out of your own way and can talk effortlessly and confidently." So I thought wouldn't it be great if there was a process, a method that helped others "get out of their own way" in their career to deliver a winning performance 365 days a year?

So, firstly, let us consider the interference question. We all strive for success in some way or another. Hands up who doesn't want to be successful by the way? Just checking…

When you remove interference you can emulate the success of others without being weighed down by a rucksack full of useless stuff. Stuff like toxic relationships, a lifestyle that is damaging to your health, unresolved personal issues, bad memories about failure or missed opportunities or poor habits that impact on your effectiveness at work (i.e. poor time management, file management, poor communication, leadership or communication skills).

Then there's other stuff like low self-esteem or no belief in yourself or your ability. Everything will be stuffed in that rucksack you are carrying, and each year it gets heavier and heavier slowing down your progress. For some people their entire existence revolves around what's in the sack until they've forgotten the carefree days before it's existence! Some people proudly hang onto that rucksack until they are almost joined at the hip!

Let's turn to science to illustrate what interference does. Imagine switching on a radio; occasionally interference will affect the reception as the following diagram will illustrate.

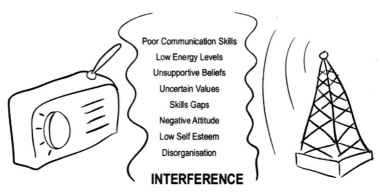

Poor Communication Skills
Low Energy Levels
Unsupportive Beliefs
Uncertain Values
Skills Gaps
Negative Attitude
Low Self Esteem
Disorganisation

INTERFERENCE

Eliminate the interference and the transmission comes across loud and clear! I worked with someone once who had so much 'interference' going on, that when we removed it all – she looked 10 years younger!

"I shall seize Fate by the throat; it shall certainly not bend and crush me completely."
Ludwig van Beethoven

THE STRENGTH OF SOFT SKILLS

These days, anyone who has a career - and that includes most men and women - knows that they have to take charge of their own Continual Professional Development (CPD), to arm themselves with the right skills to be a better leader, build stronger relationships and handle themselves with more confidence and assurance.

Paradoxically it's the soft skills which will be essential in order for you to survive this brave new world. As more and more people are required to navigate uncertain career paths towards self-employment, innovation and entrepreneurialism (and possibly re-invent themselves over and over), key soft skills (emotional intelligence) will be required to give them a head start to make them more employable.

Neil Scrotton, President UK International Coach Federation says, *"I believe we are at a vital point in our history. The challenges facing us as individuals and as a global community are huge. The decisions and actions we take now will be crucial. Coaching is becoming massive in the world – and I believe for a reason – great positive change needs to happen. What we do as coaches this year, be it working at an individual level on personal change, or with a corporate on a global scale, has the potential to literally change the world. There is nothing we can do that is either too small or too large – it all has the potential to help. There is no individual or organisation we can work with that does not have a part to play– no-one should be excluded. This is a challenge and an incredible privilege... The world is calling us – the time is now. Let's make something good happen."*

"The real source of wealth and capital in this new era is not material things. It is the human mind, the human spirit, the human imagination, and our faith in the future."
Steve Forbes, Billionaire Publisher

HOW TO GET THE MOST OUT OF THE 7 CORE PRINCIPLES

1. Highlight those phrases and paragraphs which resonate strongly with you.

2. There are personal workshop activities to help you get to grips with this material and an Appendix which contains a 90 Day Action Plan for you to execute some of these changes.

3. Get a notebook and start writing down your thoughts. Use it to get the most out of this material.

4. Share this with someone who will champion and support your progress.

5. Keep it somewhere where you will have easy access to it every day.

I have included a list of recommended reading at the end of this book. So, if you're ready? Let's get going...

Principle 1 - Environment

"Brain cells create ideas. Stress kills brain cells. Stress is not a good idea."
Frederick Saunders, American librarian and essayist (1807-1902)

Poor Environment + Lifestyle + Routine = Stress

Definition of an Environment: external surroundings in which a plant or animal lives, which influences its development and behaviour.

For anything to survive and thrive it will require a beneficial nurturing and supportive environment.

Examples of an environment include:

- The Office
- Your Car
- Your Support Network
- Your Co-Workers
- Your Study
- Your Garden
- Your Home
- Your Body
- Your Finances

DOES YOUR ENVIRONMENT SUPPORT YOU?

Imagine you are a fish swimming around in an aquarium. How important would a healthy environment be to your wellbeing?

Imagine you see another fish which unfortunately has a tumour. To cure the problem, we here in the West would probably remove the fish, cut out the tumour and then put it right back into the aquarium, and never even consider that it might have been the environment that caused the illness. We tend only to look at the symptoms, and take remedial action.

Eastern cultures however, look at things differently. They would remove the fish, clean the aquarium, provide fresh water and then return the fish. The only reason that the fish became sick in the first place was because the water the fish was swimming in was toxic and therefore unable to sustain the fish long term.

Now take your office for instance. This is an environment which has to contain the right elements in order to maximise your efficiency and also support your wellbeing. Your office environment contains so many elements and usually refers to your support network (including people) the set-up at home (if you work from home) e.g. desk, heating, lighting, filing space and storage, as well as your systems and procedures. Other environments would also support your finances and even your health. These should all contribute towards your enhanced effectiveness, productively and peace of mind. Get the environments that govern these areas in good working order and you will lay strong foundations on which to build on your success.

Now problems with stress and health issues have their roots in the following:

- Lack of self-discipline.
- Roles/Job Descriptions not defined clearly enough.
- Inability to prioritise or say no.
- Lack of systems and processes.
- Reluctance to delegate.
- Cramming too much into your schedule.
- Underestimating the time it takes to get a task completed.
- Being distracted by new stuff.
- Interruptions and not re-prioritising.
- Poor lifestyle choices and habits.

Therefore developing new habits will help you reduce stress and become more productive. Once you've got control over these, you've potentially eliminated a large proportion of your stress. How can you possibly, be really effective if your own workstation or office looks like a bomb just fell on it, you're not eating healthily and aren't disciplined as far as your time is concerned? Could you welcome the credibility which comes with putting your house in order? What would that bring you?

So where do you start?

First of all, look around you. You could begin to cultivate new habits, set up systems and procedures that will create an environment where you will thrive.

For example let's consider Dan 'Scarecrow' Burnside (a confirmed workaholic and adrenaline junkie). He doesn't have an off switch and keeps taking on more and more before completing the tasks that he has already undertaken.

He may use displacement activity to avoid making decisions or to face circumstances that make him feel uncomfortable because he:

- Needs to feel useful to others.
- Wants to feel important and worthy.
- Finds it impossible to delegate.
- Wants to remain in control.
- Doesn't like saying no.
- Is easily distracted.

Consequently he has become a crazed hamster on a treadmill. This has created stress and made him difficult to live or work with.

Small business owners for instance, often don't realise that when they work from home they have to be more disciplined with their time management. They need an effective support structure and systems to help them be more efficient. However in the admin arena they may be completely clueless because when they were an employee and worked for a larger organisation, they were supported by staff who took care of all their admin for them. Whereas if they run a business from home (and also have a family) then they may have conflicting priorities which drain their energy e.g. "Should I put the washing on or do some cold calling?" or "I can't focus on this report because the house hasn't been vacuumed for 7 days", or "I've spent all morning on the phone and haven't got a thing done!"

So what follows are some strategies to get yourself organised. This also introduces an element of extreme self-care. What do I mean by extreme self-care?

Self care means putting yourself first. Sounds obvious doesn't it? But when you look after yourself you have more to give. If you neglect your own needs you will eventually become so stressed and frazzled you will have nothing left in the tank, and won't be much use to anyone, let alone yourself. But some people (particularly women) find it excruciatingly hard to put themselves before everyone else.

"I'm not afraid of her. I'm not afraid of anything - except a lighted match."
The Scarecrow, The Wizard of Oz

So first things first, let's start with something easy by turning our attention to your workstation...

WHAT DOES YOUR DESK SAY ABOUT YOU?

In a recent article from *www.sedona*.com entitled "Is a tidy desk is a sign of a sick mind?" it's argued that some individuals think that those people whose desks are neat and organised could not possibly be mentally sane, while those with clean desks swear it's the only way to work.

Does it really matter whether you work to an orderly system or have no regard whatsoever to orderliness? And what does that say about you? In the article it refers to an actual syndrome called Irritable Desk Syndrome (IDS) which is associated with working long hours and having poor posture.

"Studies have shown that the person who works with a messy desk spends, on average, one-and-a-half hours per day looking for things or being distracted by things. That's seven-and-a-half hours per week," says time management speaker and consultant Dr. Donald E. Wetmore.

Moderately disorganised people tend to be more creative and more efficient and resilient than people who are extremely organised, which may actually be quite beneficial. Conversely, spending too much time keeping everything in order can become a bit of an obsession and may waste time and can be restrictive.

I think that there are benefits both for and against being excessively tidy or untidy, it does very much depend on your personality and where you place your priorities. There's no point in feeling that you 'should' have a tidy workspace, if that's not your style, but on the other hand some moderation could be applied if you know that things could get out of hand if no control is taken over your workstation.

There is another aspect to 'the desk' which can influence how effective and creative you are in coming up with solutions to problems.

According to Robert Updegraff in his article 'Desk Bound Thinking' he says: *"Desk bound thinking is probably responsible for more poor plans and decisions than is lack of business judgement. Certainly, it is responsible for the slow progress of most businesses, and for the paucity of fresh ideas and original policies. I believe that one reason Henry Ford has been able to evolve so many original and revolutionary policies is that for years he has seldom used a desk, but does his thinking on his feet, wherever he happens to be."*

You may not realise this but a lot of your important thinking and planning gets done during your commute or walk to work. It's the time spent away from your desk which is where your subconscious is able to cook up a solution, while you are still consciously going about your day. You load up your mind with conscious thoughts, rational and logical thinking so the subconscious mind to go to work on at a much deeper level.

Have you ever come up with a great new idea while you were cleaning your teeth, or were out on the golf course? A big light bulb moment for finishing this book came to me on a freezing December afternoon whilst cleaning my car! Updegraff goes onto say, *"This fireless-cooking principle is the basis of the six-hour day for executives. Six hours of conscious cooking, then put everything in the fireless to cook until done – perhaps three hours later, or three days or three weeks or three years. No need to worry; if the cooking has been started right the solution will eventually generate enough steam to blow off the lid. Out will come the solution, and with it a conviction of its rightness that will make it doubly potent."*

So, look after your desk, but don't spend too much time there...

Do I Practise What I Preach?

It's all very well telling you to go sort out that pile of filing that's been hanging around since 1984, if I'm sitting here writing this book surrounded by chaos. And I have to confess I'm not a saint! I would say that I fit into the 'moderately disorganised' category. I have a major purge every few months to ensure things don't get out of control.

I run my coaching practice from home and 18 months ago it became increasingly difficult to keep track of everything, locate important documents, prioritise or even think straight! I'd be tripping over the piles of lever arch files and folders littering the floor. Stationery was all over the place, and my books were in disarray: "Man alive, where did that box of utility bills dating back to 1999 come from?" I wasn't giving my coaching business the respect it deserved by working in a very unproductive (and unprofessional) environment.

I took the bull by the horns and called in a professional de-cluttering company.

De-cluttering was the catalyst for getting a host of other things sorted as well, such as a memory upgrade on my computer, finding a permanent home for my stationery and important records, and chucking out stuff I just didn't use or need any more. I knew that if I was materially or emotionally holding onto things then I wouldn't have room for new things. This was leading to stagnation and restricting the flow of energy.

Now my office looks bigger, it's calmer and the chi energy flows better. The room is just awesome! And there's even somewhere for my visitors to sit down for a cup of coffee and a chat. Hooray! Plus I've now got into the habit of clearing my desk when I finish for the day so I start the next day with a clear mind.

Here Are 23 Top Tips For Working More Efficiently

1. Sort and open your post daily: five minutes a day may be easier to find than one hour a week. Separate between 'action pile' and 'narr pile'.

2. Deal with any urgent bills or issues straight away, and then file.

3. Make a space for all 'pending' items - a place on the bureau or a file in the kitchen - and make sure it is checked every day.

4. Group meetings or visits to customers/clients together so that you aren't wasting travelling time.

5. Use your Satellite Navigation system. Enter the destination and log the travelling time required so that you can calculate precisely when you need to leave.

6. Organise your business cards – buy a big A4 diary and every time you meet someone new, staple the business card in the diary, with a little note next to it. This might seem a bit old fashioned but my friend Brett swears by this one!

7. Clearly label files and folders for all your projects, and colour code them if that helps.

8. Clear your desk at the end of each day.

9. Colour code your meetings in your Outlook Calendar or use a day planner.

10. Always prepare bags, documents and directions for the following day, the night before.

11. Use a task list. I use an A5 workbook and write down my tasks for the week every Sunday evening. Each day I use a different coloured highlighter pen

for those tasks. I cross through each task as it's completed and usually most things get done. It's a great feeling! Anything that isn't completed is carried over to the next list. Curiously there's never more than 20 items on the list each week, although any more than that I would go into overload. Sometimes the simple strategies work best!

12. Divide larger tasks into smaller ones, organise all the paperwork and prioritise – I call this planning to plan.

13. If you find it hard to stop when you get going on a project (even to eat), use a timer to bleep when time's up. Remember if you're hungry and thirsty, you won't think straight.

14. Organise your domestic arrangements if you work from home, to maximise the most of your time. Don't be a slave to the ironing, or try to be a domestic goddess by insisting that you do things the same way you always have. Ask yourself, what's more important for you to be doing right now? Get a cleaner or hire someone to clean your oven for instance, instead of doing it all yourself.

15. Think – is this the best use of my time and will it help me reach my objectives? If not, delegate it to someone else if you can afford to.

16. Use a 'save up' or 'wish list' for projects that you can't start straight away by placing a concertina folder close at hand for your projects and documents so you can find them.

17. Schedule your shredding! Organise a shredding basket, and allocate a designated time to shred, or shred daily rather than leaving it all to pile up.

18. Tear off the address panel from letters and instead of shredding the whole letter, just shred the address!

19. Designate a 'recycling facility' in your garage to sort the paper, tin, bottles, cardboard, paper, newspaper and recycle little and often.

20. Use only one diary, better still use an electronic diary system on your phone that synchronises with your computer on a daily basis – e.g. a ~~Blackberry.~~ *google calendar*

21. If you're having trouble sleeping, rather than lay there feeling anxious, switch the light on or get out of bed and do some planning, write an article, write some lists, brainstorm. Once you've downloaded your thoughts onto paper, you'll soon fall back to sleep!

22. At the beginning of each year, sit down with your spouse and plan your time together, e.g. holidays, family events, and important anniversaries

23. Turn your spouse into a VIP – book a date with them on a regular basis and ensure that absolutely nothing else is booked in it's place

DOES YOUR LIFE NEED AN MOT?

Take a pen and paper and answer these 3 questions:

1. Are you fed-up with dealing with one
    crisis after another?

2. Would you like your day to just 'flow' better?

3. Do you sometimes wonder if being a
    chaotic person is hereditary?

Now, assuming you've answered these questions honestly, I can probably make an educated guess that you know what needs to be done, but aren't doing anything about it.

In some respects we are a bit like cars, and once a year we should all give ourselves an MOT. I always wince when the car mechanic itemises everything that's either on the blink, needs replacing or has gone altogether. However, at least it's being dealt with, and I'm not contemplating that while I'm sitting on the motorway in the snow, waiting for the RAC to come to my rescue because I didn't take good care of my car.

Everything in this chapter can be summed up very easily. All you need to pause and reflect and take stock. Give yourself a starting point and get a clearer picture.

Let me introduce you to The Clean Sweep Test. The Clean Sweep Test is a very simple set of 100 questions. All you have to do is tick some boxes. That's it. Your own personal MOT. Here's an example of some of the questions:

- My personal files, papers and receipts are neatly filed away.
- My car is in excellent condition (doesn't need mechanical work, repairs, cleaning or replacing).
- My home is neat and clean (vacuumed, closets clean, desks and tables clear, furniture in good repair, windows clean).
- My appliances, machinery and equipment work well (refrigerator, toaster, central heating, vacuum cleaner).
- My clothes are all pressed, clean and make me look great (no wrinkles, baskets of laundry, torn, out-of-date or ill- fitting clothes).
- My plants and animals are healthy (fed, watered, getting light and love).
- My bed/bedroom lets me have the best sleep possible (firm bed, light, air).

Sometimes when things get complicated, when things aren't going our way, it's because we might have developed bad habits, overlooked or ignored tasks (hoping they will go away), or haven't followed through or been proactive enough. The Clean Sweep Test is divided into 4 main areas: Physical Environment, Money, Well-Being and Relationships.

Unfortunately the things we ignore have a nasty habit of coming back and biting us on the derriere when we're least expecting it. Things start to overheat in your life, and you may spend a big chunk of your day fire-fighting. Someone I know was due to drive to the South of France and only realised his passport had run out the day before his trip. He therefore had to race to the passport office on ιe morning. Meanwhile his friend was having ~ρ..aιions waiting anxiously at the Euro Star.

The aim of the Clean Sweep Test is to get a score of 100 points. Achieving anything less than 60 points indicates you need to take a serious look at your life. Some things can be sorted out with just a letter, an e-mail or a phone call. Some will need careful planning, others might highlight an area in your life that really isn't working at all.

This exercise includes evaluating your relationships. Who could be draining your resources for example? Who's taking you for granted, or makes you so stressed it brings you out in a rash? What behaviour are you tolerating? The exercise could highlight areas where you might not be taking responsibility in some areas of your life and are relying too much on others. Well here's your chance to make some long overdue changes.

Take the Clean Sweep Test and find out what action you need to take. Highlight where you'd like to start and off you go. Stick the list on the fridge and even if you only pick one thing to concentrate on this week, you will *feel* so much better about yourself. I recommend running a Clean Sweep Test on yourself on a regular basis, in the same way that you might run an anti-virus check on your computer, or back up your files. The same rules apply.

Log onto my website to take the test at *www.resolutioncoaching.co.uk*

ARE YOU BEING ATTACKED BY
THE WINGED MONKEYS?

Now it's time to get clear on your priorities and how you use your time.

An inability to use your time properly leads to frayed tempers, mistakes and exhaustion. Running around like a headless chicken then becomes a habit, leaving no room to stop, reflect and take stock. People who run their lives, and their offices, this way are constantly running from one crisis to another.

They might take on too much, find it hard to say no or to delegate. It's hard to be effective with too many monkeys on your shoulders, demanding your attention and sapping your strength. Consequently this frenzy of activity will be stressful to everyone around them who will be at the mercy of their poor working strategy, leading to mistakes, missed deadlines and strained relationships.

One observation I have made is that some stressed-out people don't actually realise they are suffering with stress at all, until their body signals to them through an illness that they are having problems coping.

The reason for this is that they are either so used to taking care of other people that they ignore their own needs, until they get a warning sign that signals they are becoming stressed. So they turn into a grumpy person, and their bad mood becomes a habit. Each of us has a unique marker which indicates when we are stressed. Initially this marker could be recurring headaches, a minor skin complaint, digestive disorders or vague feelings of sadness or forgetfulness. Sometimes we ignore these markers and fail to take any notice of these little 'hints' that something isn't quite right, until it's too late. By then the marker has turned into a ruddy great roadblock in the form of a breakdown, heart attack or long-term chronic illness. We'll look more closely at the impact of stress on your health later.

Similarly reactive management is a huge waste of time and resources. So wouldn't you love to win the respect of those around you and stay in control instead?

If that's yes, let me help you calculate how you are using your time. If you are so busy in your life, you may not realise how long your working day or week is. I say this because whilst I was doing my coaching training I was also working full-time, and in the end I caught the flu. I missed an important exam because I was completely run down. I needed to see what my schedule was actually looking like so I logged where my time was being allocated with a time calculator. This calculates your activities in half hour increments. The total numbers of hours I was engaged in work and training came in at an exhausting 80 hours a week! No wonder I was exhausted. I realised that I had to give something up, or at least slow down a bit before I burnt out.

So, if you are running around like a headless chicken and are finding that you are robbing Peter to pay Paul as far as your time is concerned, I encourage you to do this exercise. Set some realistic boundaries around your life, so that whatever activity you are engaged in is given your full attention, as well as being enjoyable and productive. There are only 24 hours in a day. If you're cramming too much in it, the quality of your life will begin to deteriorate and you could be setting yourself up for problems later on, including chronic stress.

Your time could easily be sub-divided in the following way:

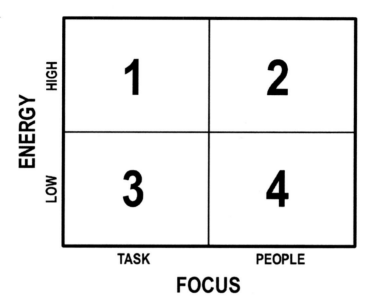

Look at the above diagram. Imagine your time is divided into quadrants, some of which are for high impact/high energy activities which are either task or people oriented, or low energy low impact activities again focussed on either people or tasks.

Taking the information from your time grid mentioned earlier you could sub-divide the time you've spent in the following ways:

1. **High Energy – Tasks**
    - Finishing a report
    - Working on a Database
    - Crisis Management
    - Walking the Dog
    - Answering e-mails

2. **High Energy – People**
    - Attending Meetings
    - Follow-up Phone Calls
    - Cold Calling
    - Staffing issues
    - Family issues (children/spouse)

3. **Low Energy – Tasks**
    - Research
    - Planning
    - Filing
    - Admin
    - Budgeting

4. **Low Energy – People**
    - Lunch meetings
    - Idle chit-chat on the phone
    - Reading Magazines
    - Watching TV
    - Sleeping

Quadrant 1 and 2 are where most of your energy will be required, although it's advisable not to spend too much time in Quadrant 1 because this will be tiring and will drain your resources. Quadrants 2 and 3 are essentially for long-term preparations and relationship building and therefore feed into the results achieved in Quadrant 1. There is no perfect scenario with regards to your time;

the key though is to create balance. If you spend too much time in one of the above 4 boxes this will have a knock on effect in the other 3. If you imagine that you have say 20 credits – 5 for each quadrant. If you start to go over your allocated credits in one box you are essentially 'borrowing' from the other 3. You can also use the quadrants to mitigate the impact felt from spending too much time in say quadrant 1, by spending some time in quadrant 4 to reduce your stress levels.

You could even say to yourself, "hey, I'm going to stay in box number 4 today and recharge", or "I've been putting some things off for too long, I need a focussed day in box number 1". Perhaps you've been neglecting the people in your life, so could benefit from allocating some quality time in box number 2 before moving onto box number 3 for some serious planning. Do you get the general idea?

Poor time management isn't the only thing that can lead to stress. A lot of stress is also linked to your personality, and how you react to stressful situations.

There are long term consequences of ignoring stress or trying to live with it. As you get older, your body will find it harder and harder to cope and will eventually start to fail. Stress exhausts vital nutrients and burns them up in huge amounts. B Vitamins and Vitamin C for instance.

Chronic stress could expose your body to unhealthy, persistently elevated levels of stress hormones like adrenaline and cortisol. Studies[1] also link stress to changes in the way blood clots, which increases the risk of heart attack.

---

[1] www.medicinenet.com

Visit my website at *www.resolutioncoaching.co.uk* and try the Clean Sweep Programme or the Adrenaline Self Test.

But before we leave the subject of time management, what if you'd love more time to achieve a big ambition which so far hasn't materialised?

Here is another important secret. Stop watching the television. If you actually added up all the hours you spend in a year watching TV, you'd be amazed. Unfortunately, the average person, according to the most recent figures from Nielsen Media Research Inc., watches TV for 4 hours and 35 minutes every single day. Worse, the average household has a TV playing for 8 hours 14 minutes every day. That's nearly 3,000 hours a year or 125 days! Switch the TV off and only prioritise programmes that you really want to watch, instead of watching television because it's there!

So, what does stress actually do to your body...?

HEALTH

If you were totally honest and knew that your lifestyle was unhealthy, you could in fact be committing crimes against your stomach.

A poor diet and eating habits, excessive drinking and smoking contribute towards stress and could be the cause of indigestion, IBS leading to a poor uptake of vital vitamins and minerals thus creating lower energy levels. The western fast food culture and the consumption of foods grown in depleted soils, means that generally western nations are not very healthy, even though we have supermarkets full of food! Plus factory farming and the over-use of antibiotics, pesticides and herbicides all contribute to our health problems.

Unfortunately, the conventional answer to stress has up until recently, relied more on prescription drugs which although they are prescribed to cure, are actually not very good for your health! For instance, antibiotics wipe out friendly bacteria in the gut alongside the bad and also destroy essential vitamins and minerals including B vitamins, magnesium, Vitamin A , zinc and iron.

According to Paul Zane Pilzer in his book 'The Wellness Revolution', "...*until the relatively recent invention of the electron microscope which is still not as widespread as the optical microscope was in the 1800s, scientists were unable to study the molecular structure of cells and how they function. This led most Western medical school training to virtually ignore, to this day, the importance of nutrition and the effects of vitamins, minerals and natural supplements.*"

I know, because as a migraine sufferer from the age of 14, I've tried everything medically to cure this, and I am now more or less allergic or resistant to all painkillers and antibiotics. What I didn't know was that the migraine drugs were slowly damaging my digestion and depleting my body of essential vitamins and minerals. Eventually the penny dropped when I realised that it was a lifestyle/food thing so I then made some long overdue changes. Drinking Aloe Vera Gel cured the problem.

But here's a curious observation.

Some people mistakenly think that if they are feeling a bit fed-up or lack motivation it's because they have a deep-seated problem which needs serious therapy, when in fact it may have more to do with what they're eating (or not eating!)

Let me give you an example. About 20 years ago I was rushed into hospital with suspected appendicitis. Waiting 4 hours for a consultant triggered a migraine. When I was discharged two days later and got back to work, I was given a book by one of the guys in the office called 'Not all in the Mind'. I looked at him as if he were bonkers.

On reading this book I discovered that I was actually allergic to coffee! Prior to this I had experienced palpitations and all sorts of unexplained symptoms, and generally felt very panicky all the time. I probably drank about 10 cups of coffee a day when I was at work. However, I'd go 'cold turkey' at weekends when I didn't drink any coffee at all and every Saturday I would develop a migraine (colossal headache, nausea and vomiting. I'd get the shakes and my lips would turn blue). Once I realised what was happening to me I replaced the coffee with water. I took my own bottled water to work with me, because back in 1981 a water cooler wasn't standard issue in offices. To be absolutely truthful, in the first few weeks' drinking water made me gag, but eventually my taste buds got used to the taste and I actually started to enjoy it! I haven't drank coffee at work now for over 25 years, but once a month I treat myself to a cappuccino, which I love; but water is so much better for my brain! I love it!

Sometimes we may experience unexplained symptoms such as mood swings or depression that we can't quite put our finger on. We might convince ourselves that there's some deep psychological problem lurking in our psyche that needs months of counselling to deal with. Take a closer look at your complexion, and your eyes. What colour is your tongue, and what do your joints feel like? Someone who glows from the inside usually glows from the outside as well. All you need to do is change your eating habits, cut out the rubbish and drink more water. Sometimes the clues really are right under your nose!

A healthy digestive system creates the right conditions for an improved uptake of vitamins and minerals, which in turn supercharges your immune system and boosts your ability to function and think properly. So treat your digestion as another 'environment' that needs to be nurtured. A robust immune system also makes you fitter, stronger and therefore more resilient to stress.

If you're serious about improving your health, here is what you need to do. Firstly carry out an audit of your fridge and throw out all the stuff that's bad for your health (processed, fatty foods, and anything high in sugar and salt for instance), commence a food diary and begin to make some minor changes to your eating habits.

I don't advocate going on a crash diet and advise caution at this point, as we all know what happens when you decide to go on a starvation diet, only to give up a week later.

Are You Sending Yourself On A Guilt Trip Over Food?

Paradoxically, one of the things that prevents people doing anything about their lifestyle or weight problems is guilt. They may feel miserable about some aspects of their life, spend even more time beating themselves up about their bad habits and feel so de-motivated as a result that they resort to eating even more comfort food – it's a vicious circle. I'd go as far as to say that diets shouldn't even be called diets. In fact, going on a diet might be bad for your health if undertaken incorrectly.

Traditionally diets focus on denial and forcing yourself to go to the gym to punish yourself on the rowing machine, when you hate rowing! I know people who loath exercise, so they pay for the membership to the gym and never turn up; and isn't it funny that when you're on a diet and the only thing you're allowed to eat is a salad, you spend all day dreaming about a McDonalds or chocolate instead?

Wouldn't it be kinder to you if you just took yourself off for a brisk walk after dinner every evening and thought more about making some minor dietary changes? Feels easier, doesn't it? I know someone who lost two stone just doing that. What I am recommending here is designing a balanced eating plan that fits in with your lifestyle. It's completely do-able and one that you can stick to.

Think about making one tiny change a week by trying some of the following:

- Replace unhealthy foods with healthy alternatives rather than cutting all the goodies out altogether.
- Cut down on tea and coffee and drink more water.
- Eat only when you're hungry.
- Identify what triggers binge eating and if there is an emotional reason then deal with it (EFT helps here – see the info later in the book on EFT).
- Chew your food s-l-o-w-l-y.
- Remove temptation. If you don't want to eat any more chocolate or biscuits, then don't have them in the house.

- Reward yourself once a week with something you really love eating.
- Walk more, for example by taking the stairs rather than the lift.
- Cut down on alcohol or only drink at weekends
- Stop smoking and take up a sport instead
- Eat what you want, but don't pile food on your plate (or use a smaller plate ...)

Now if you're really serious about improving your health, log onto www.patrickholford.com

Patrick Holford is a pioneer in new approaches to health and nutrition, specialising in the field of mental health. He is widely regarded as Britain's best-selling author and leading spokesman on nutrition and mental health issues, and is frequently quoted in national newspapers from the *Daily Mail* to the *Guardian*. Patrick is also popular on radio shows and national television as a presenter, interviewer and guest.

STOP THE WORLD I WANT TO GET OFF! ADVICE FOR WORKAHOLIC ADRENALINE JUNKIES...

If your workload or career is pushing your stress levels through the roof, then what follows is a simple guide to how your brain works. I know because, being a borderline adrenaline junkie, I've had to learn some of these strategies myself to stay balanced. Believe me, this stuff really works!

Do you remember when you were a kid and the summer holidays seemed to last forever? You invented games to play from the most innocuous and mundane objects, which became holy shrines or magic keys. Drinks turned you into a superhero. Up until the age of 10, that is.

That's because before the age of 10, children primarily use the right hemisphere of their brain - the creative side. The creative right side of the brain produces Alpha waves, and when you meditate, your brain produces more Alpha waves. In Alpha we naturally have a better command of life, our health and our moods. We are able to think more clearly, can consider responses and perhaps make more creative decisions, with better long-term results. Alpha thought waves help us to access that part of the brain responsible for more enlightened, sophisticated thinking.

John Levine composes Alpha Music to help people relax and is used by Complementary Therapists to help their clients easily produce Alpha waves and therefore enter a deep state of relaxation very quickly. I was introduced to this music by a therapist friend, and regularly listen to this when I am brainstorming, writing when relaxing or meditating. It's extraordinarily serene.

According to Levine research shows that when we're in Alpha through to Theta (as we prepare to go to sleep), the brain also produces a number of chemical hormones which affect our mood, productivity and general health. Delta waves then take over as we fall into slow wave (deep sleep).

However, after the age of 10 different brain waves take over - Beta waves. Beta waves vibrate at a higher frequency and are linked with the left logical side of the brain. Coincidentally this is when children move on to secondary school, where everything gets really 'serious'. Gone are the lazy days spent fishing for newts and making mud pies (by the way if you didn't made mud pies when you were a kid – you haven't lived!). Now it's all homework, course modules, mock exams, routines and remembering loads of facts – fun, eh? Leaving precious little time for imaginative thinking, talking or creative pastimes, which could lead to stress.

Levine also discovered that although Beta waves are important, if this is the dominant thought wave, we remain hyped-up and stressed. So being in this state is not good long term. We are less likely to make rational choices and our responses are more primitive as higher thinking begins to shut down. However, some people appear to be born with a gift for increased Alpha wave production. Scientists have established that creative people operate in Alpha and Theta states far more frequently than the rest of us.

Eventually we leave school to start a career, with the accompanying train timetables, spreadsheets, passwords e-mails and compliance, etc. All logical left brain stuff and yet more Beta brain activity.

In fact bringing your creative streak out in a work environment (in some organisations) is positively frowned upon and discouraged. Until, that is, you wake up one morning and wonder why you haven't a single scrap of innovation left in you. You can't switch off because you're so stressed-out having to reach all your 'targets'. As Daniel Goleman in his book "Emotional Intelligence" puts it *"Stress Makes You Stupid"*.

With all that Beta brain activity going on, there's just no inspiration or fun in your life any more. Using 'Beta' thought waves too often is like driving your car everywhere in first gear. Being grown up and serious has actually become really stressful. All the routine, discipline and targets haven't actually made you any more effective or indeed any happier. Need I say more?

This is where you may become even less effective, shut off from the 'source' – the source being the pipeline leading directly to all new ideas and innovation: your creative right brain. Although it is important to point out that you need a good balance between the left and right sides.

"Experiments show that most children rank highly creative (right brain) before entering school. Because our educational systems place a higher value on left brain skills such as mathematics, logic and language than it does on drawing or using our imagination, only ten percent of these same children will rank highly creative by age 7. By the time we are adults, high creativity remains in only 2 percent of the population."

Dan Eden, editor, viewzone.com

Early signs of stress include being a bit tetchy, food cravings, mood swings, feeling extremely tired or hyped-up leading to sleep problems caused by too much Beta brainwave activity and stress hormones racing around your bloodstream.

Long-term stress will have disastrous consequences for your health. As you get older, your body will find it harder and harder to cope and could be the reason why some people are struck down with chronic conditions such as arthritis, chronic fatigue, IBS, High Blood

Pressure, and raised levels of cholesterol. The short-term solution is treatment with conventional drugs, when in fact the long term and ultimately the best solution is to give your lifestyle a complete overhaul.

Not paying attention to your stress levels and lifestyle, affects your body, your energy levels, and your resistance to stress. Ultimately, your ability to rationalise and memorise, and your performance at work will suffer.

If this rings any bells with you, then it's time to balance your brain.

15 Tips For Getting Into The Alpha State

1. Take some time out and listen to 'Alpha Music' *www.silenceofmusic.com*
2. Go for a long walk and switch off at least three times a week.
3. Watch a film that makes you laugh.
4. Learn to meditate or try Reiki.
5. Have a massage.
6. Have a soak in the bath.
7. Get yourself organised and delegate.
8. Shift down a gear and get away from your computer and meet someone for coffee - schedule some 'me' time.
9. Start saying no to unreasonable demands, and don't turn up for events that you just don't want to attend.
10. Schedule time for 'naff' activities – e.g. tidying up. Apparently Margaret Thatcher used to sort out the laundry cupboards and do low level activities to reduce stress.

11. Start a hobby, i.e. golf, tennis, dancing, singing.

12. Educate yourself in good sleep 'hygiene' i.e. going to bed at a reasonable time and allowing yourself to wind down for half an hour before you go to sleep.

13. Don't keep a computer or a TV in your bedroom.

14. Build a strong network of supporters around you who you can share your concerns or worries with.

15. Don't watch TV (especially horror movies) late at night. In fact, limit TV altogether.

Now while you're in the Alpha wave phase - just being a big kid – you will create a lava flow of ideas and inspiration. Not only will that generate more energy, you'll get more done, you will feel so much happier and your day will flow more easily. You will get through more tasks in less time, and be fully 'present' at work completely engaged and in the zone.

"If as children we constantly secrete large quantities of cortisol to make us ready for 'fight-or-flight' in the face of parental maltreatment, it can cause permanent brain damage making us hyper-responsive to seemingly innocuous events: panic or anxiety, or a collapse of self-esteem, are very easily triggered. Infants of depressed mothers, and those who have been abused or neglected, have heightened levels of stress hormones such as cortisol. Brain scans reveal abnormal patterns of brainwaves in the frontal lobes, and right side of the brain, which is associated with depression in adults."
Oliver James, 'They F*** You Up – How to Survive Family Life'

LET'S TALK ABOUT YOUR FINANCES

Your finances are another support environment which if not watched closely may become a burden rather than a supporter for you. From my own experiences I know it has always been important for me to be proactive in this area. Each year it is always worthwhile running an audit of your expenditure to evaluate what's working well for you or what may need amending. Here is a short checklist of statements concerning finances to get you thinking:

- I pay my bills on time, virtually always.
- My income source/revenue base is stable and predictable.
- I know how much I must have to be minimally financially independent and I have a plan to get there.
- I live on a weekly budget that allows me to save and not suffer.
- All my tax returns have been filed and all my taxes have been paid.
- I currently live well, within my means.
- My assets (car, home, possessions, treasures) are well-insured.
- I have a financial plan for the next year.
- My will is up-to-date and accurate.
- Any parking tickets, alimony or child support are paid and current.
- My investments do not keep me awake at night.
- I know how much I am worth.

Another side to this is that money is a source of energy. Much of what I've talked about in this book is essentially about the flow of energy. Focusing your energies on a definite plan of action (as I will explain later in the book) works towards creating success, the natural consequence of which, is money.

Therefore, being organised and efficient, discovering your true path and putting together a plan to get you there will bring you closer to financial security.

Managing Debt

Currently as this book is going to print, the global economic outlook is extremely depressing and many countries have gone into a recession. The crisis in the banking industry has had a catastrophic impact on manufacturing and service industries. Many businesses have gone to the wall leading to mass redundancies. At a personal level this has created enormous problems for families, particularly with rising levels of personal debt. Thousands of families are struggling to make ends meet leading to depression and anxiety. If you fall into this category there are some key recommendations to help you move through this situation and develop a strategy to move forward:

1.   Be proactive. If you notice that things are sliding out of control and you can't meet your commitments take the initiative and get in touch with a debt management company. Look at the resource list at the end of this book for more information.

2.   Talking this through with a finance professional significantly helps to reduce the anxiety. Some of these organisations can take over negotiations with your creditors for you so you aren't stressed out with the constant phone calls and letters.

3.   If you take action early by getting in touch with your creditors you are far more likely to successfully manage the situation before things get out of control.

4.   If there is only a minor short-fall look at ways of plugging the gap with some part-time or short term work.

5.   What treats that you have taken for granted could you actually give up? You could reduce consumption of take-away food, cancel subscriptions to magazines, run a car that is more fuel efficient, turn the heating down and wear more jumpers in the winter.

6.   Look at ways of consolidating your debt so that it is more manageable.

7.   Look at the skills that you have that you could turn into a useful source of additional income.

8.   Being proactive and taking action does a lot for your morale.

For anyone running a business here are some top tips on creating long-term financial security and stability:

Stabilise

1.   Stabilise your business so that you have a good foundation upon which to grow.

2.   Survive on lower sales – know your breakeven point. What factors influence breakeven and what do you need to do to take back control?

3.   Increase prices – you cannot compete with larger companies on price so use your price as a positive differentiator. Pricing also impacts

on your breakeven point by increasing your gross profit margin.

4. Cut direct costs – what should you cut first to minimize any detrimental effects on the long-term viability of your business? Cutting direct cost will increase your gross profit margin and reduce your breakeven point.

5. Cut overheads – what should you cut first? If your overheads are lower then your breakeven point can also be lower.

6. Slow down cash outgoings – businesses can be profitable yet still go bust through lack of cash, so how can you slow down your necessary cash outgoings without losing credit facilities from suppliers?

7. Speed up the collection of cash – most people hate collecting cash in from customers but this is one area you really must get right to stay in business.

8. Financing your business – sometimes a business simply cannot generate sufficient working capital from its own resources and needs to look to outside finance. The secret here is to do it before you need it.

9. Management information – most businesses which go bust have poor management accounting information so make sure you have robust accounting systems which are accurate and up to date.

Analyse

Now you need to properly understand both yourself and your business.

1. Personal strengths and weaknesses – do you really have what it takes to run your own business? If you don't then get a job.

2. SWOT analysis – carry out a SWOT analysis on your business. This means Strengths, Weaknesses, Opportunities and Threats.

3. Understand your figures – not much point in having management accounts if you do not understand what they mean. Get your accountant to explain them in detail to you.

4. Financial analysis – this involves more than looking at a profit and loss account. It means finding out what your KPIs (Key Performance Indicators) are and constantly monitoring them.

Capitalise

Now that you have stabilised the business and really understand what makes it tick you can capitalise on the strong foundations you have built. This is the marketing phase.

1. Market research – don't try to sell something your customers either don't want or would like but don't want to pay for it. Do your research properly or better still get someone else to do it for you.

2. Increase the number of customers – there are lots of ways to do this but you need to focus on the ones which work and work consistently.

3.   Help your customers buy more often – your existing customers should be encouraged to come back to buy more often.

4.   Increase the average transaction value – your existing customers should be encouraged to spend more when they visit you.

5.   Increase customer retention – preventing customers from going elsewhere is cheaper and more effective than trying to poach customers from competitors. Look after what you have already got.

Revolutionise

Standing still is no longer an option, you need to change to cope with the way business will be done in the future.

1.   Strategic planning – this has consistently been used for decades by big businesses to achieve success. Strategic planning is much more than a simple business plan. You can also achieve more if you use an outside expert to help you develop.

2.   Improve the efficiency of processes – systems, systems and more systems. It's a simple fact that what gets measured improves. If you don't have systems you have nothing to measure against and therefore nothing improves.

3.   Customer service – this is usually what differentiates a small business from a big business. It is usually the simple things such as respect for the customer, a smile, going the extra mile. During the credit crunch this will make the biggest difference to your success.

4.   Buying other businesses – you are profitable with cash in the bank so now what? Expand by buying those businesses which will complement your own? Now would be a great time to buy another business.

What the 'credit crunch' has shown us is that the pace of change is always accelerating and we cannot afford to be complacent. Although there may currently be more risks for the uneducated there are greater opportunities for the knowledgeable. The key to success today more than ever before is having the 'knowledge'. The knowledge of how businesses really work and not just the technical knowledge about a product or a service.

Source information: Wood & Disney Chartered Accountants *www.wood-disney.co.uk*

ARE YOU FACING CHANGE?

Change is sometimes a choice, but for some people change may have been forced on them through redundancy, illness or retirement. The material in this book will be particularly relevant if the skills that you've grown accustomed to using in your role have themselves become redundant.

Some professionals link their identity to their career and forget that it's not them that's been made redundant, it's their role, their job. If there is a lot of status attached to their role, then they may feel the loss of both the job and the status that went with it. This could create a high level of anxiety or even a feeling of failure. Redundancy also affects people at a social level, when their routine changes meaning they lose contact with their peers and social/support network. Plus of course redundancy could place a strain on their finances.

For some people the transition from where they are now to where they want to be can be a bit of an odyssey. However, when disaster strikes we could be lured into thinking that 'this is how it is' and things will never change. Once you start to think like that well it's 'game over'. But any change follows a distinct pattern.

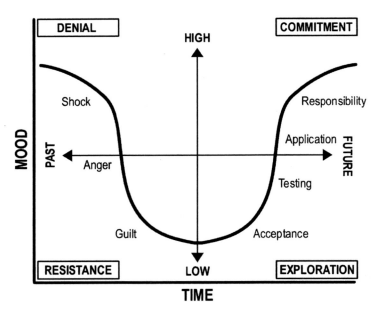

This diagram is known as the 'grief curve'. It represents the stages that each of us goes through when facing change or experience a feeling of loss. We normally associate the word grief with the death or loss someone close to us. When experiencing a period of change, I think it is helpful to recognise that you needn't stand still but you must move on. There are very specific staging points and feelings associated with this process. It begins with shock, anger and resentment (which keep us stuck in the past) and eventually moving upwards towards hope and excitement as the future beckons.

If you are currently facing change recognise that you are moving through this curve. Notice that eventually change does lead to something positive. Complications arise if you aren't prepared to move forward and are thus mired in inertia and powerlessness.

> *"And I was standing over there rusting*
> *for the longest time."*
> **The Tin Man, The Wizard of Oz**

At a career level even success and advancement represents change and gaining a promotion can be challenging. So by recognising that change is a process, the whole experience could be more meaningful and endurable.

In surveys only 52% of employers provide coaching/training to staff affected by change, yet a recent survey found 99% of employers believe coaching can deliver tangible benefits to both individuals and organisations.

Look at the grief curve and place a mark along the curve which indicates where you are at this present moment on your own personal journey...

TIME FOR A BRAIN DUMP

The Wheel of Life

To help you see the bigger picture of your life both personally and professionally I recommend the following activity, called The Wheel of Life. I sometimes refer to it as a 'brain dump'. You unpack everything in your mind, a bit like dismantling a car engine, then systematically put it back together again. So if there's more going on than just pure time management or organisational/procedures stuff, then this exercise is very useful. Let me elaborate.

You may have other issues to contend with in your career, like frustrating work colleagues, commuting, legislation, litigation, reaching retirement, redundancy, family commitments, or problems with your finances or health. The list is endless. You might be planning to emigrate, go on an expedition to South America, write a book, change career directions, study or walk to the North Pole. This same coaching model can be applied to literally anything.

This is how it works. Imagine your challenge as a big wheel or pie, which can be divided into slices. The pie can comprise anything from 6, 8 or even 10 slices - it depends on each individual.

The slices of your pie could include the following:

- Finances
- Relationships
- Time Management
- Self-Confidence
- Career Objectives
- Training
- Health
- Spiritual development

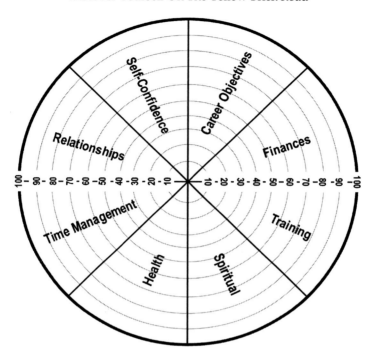

Evaluate each slice on a scale of 1-10 (10 = Fantastic 0 = Poor). Then choose the top three to work on first. Some slices of the pie link together and sometimes work undertaken in one area will have a domino effect on some of the others. This activity will help you develop and prioritise new solutions and strategies. Funnily enough when I give my clients permission to take an in-depth look at their life, they do find it very cathartic. It takes a weight off their mind to get some clarity at long last.

So imagine your challenge as a pie and divide it into slices using this diagram. Then pick the top three 'slices' you'd like to work on first and mark a star next to these. You can go back to this diagram again and again to review your progress.

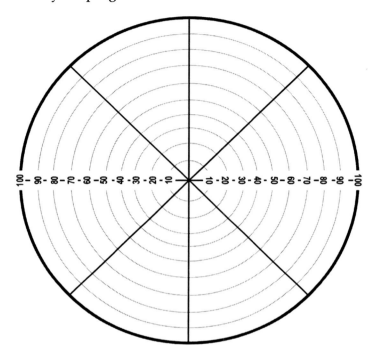

Now Get Out Of That

The Wheel of Life exercise isn't just confined to individuals. It can be applied to teams as well and used as a brainstorming tool.

I facilitated a brainstorming session for my local networking group, The Business Café (www.businesscafe.biz). They were looking to attract more visitors and grow the membership. I introduced this very simple coaching model to them and expanded on the process. Using the mastermind principle I was hopeful that their 'collective minds' would work together to harness the power of synergy. My job was as the facilitator to challenge and encourage interaction.

The result of this was that almost immediately once some of the new ideas were implemented, the group started to attract new visitors and from 16 members this grew to 32 and is still going strong!

ACTION POINTS - ENVIRONMENT

1. What practical steps do you need to take to smarten up your environment, lifestyle, office space, finances, routine processes and procedures?
2. Take steps to identify them individually.
3. Deal with, get support on or delegate some of your projects or tasks.
4. Create an action plan, decide to decide and take action.

Environment Power Question
How will being more organised affect the wider systems you belong to?

Dan sat back and reflected on how he was running his life. He resolved to go home, talk things over with his wife and use the Christmas holidays to re-think his whole lifestyle. He also needed to jettison some responsibilities that he was reluctant to delegate and stop trying to win brownie points all the time. He also decided to look after himself a bit better. This was a hard lesson, but if he carried on the way he was – he'd be dead by the time he reached 40.

Tom had never compared his office to a fish tank, but when he did he could clearly identify who the sharks were! There were shoals of plankton, definitely a few angel fish and a couple of turtles, but what was Tom? He didn't fit the description of a barracuda. Perhaps he was a dolphin? Nice, friendly but always getting caught up in the tuna nets. Was the sea that he inhabited really the best environment for him in which to thrive and reach his potential? His office was fine if you were a killer whale or a box jellyfish, but if you weren't - you were just dinner.

He needed to swim to more friendly waters.

Louisa looked around the carriage as she reached the end of the first principle. She was so diligent, she'd forgotten to reach out to her colleagues and form any strong supportive relationships or even allow those above her to see her potential. They had assumed she was doing OK, or didn't really need her friendship. This had turned her into a bit of a loner, and cannon fodder for the wicked witch of the west. Although she wasn't quite sure how she was going to turn herself into a people magnet over night, but at least she was more aware that a course correction was required.

Principle 2 - Capabilities

"Years ago, one of my teachers, Jim Rohn, taught me that reading something of substance, something of value, something that was nurturing, something that taught you new distinctions every day, was more important than eating. He got me hooked on the idea of reading a minimum of thirty minutes a day. He said 'miss a meal, but don't miss your reading'."
Anthony Robbins, Motivational Speaker

Capabilities include:

- Technical
- Leadership
- Communication
- Organisational
- Management
- Creative
- Thinking & Analysis
- Manual Dexterity
- Sales
- Networking

GETTING INTO THE FLOW

University of Chicago psychologist Mihaly Csikszentmihalyi researched the psychology of 'flow' for 20 years and studied the accounts of athletes who had experienced peak performance and were able to get themselves into 'the zone'. Entry into 'the zone' can occur when people find a task they are skilled at and engage in, at a level that slightly taxes their ability. Flow occurs in that delicate zone between boredom and anxiety when the demands on them are a bit greater than usual and they are able to give a little more. If there is too little demand on them, people are bored. If there is too much for them to handle, they get anxious.

Have you ever tried something and failed dismally at it? Or been in a position where nobody understood you and you felt like you were bashing your head against a brick wall?

How was your self-esteem? I can probably guess that it was a bit low, not exactly guaranteed to turn you into a trailblazer...

Now, think about a time where everything just flowed. Was everything so easy that you almost felt guilty about it? Effortless results followed and you felt buoyant and confident. You were decisive and in control, and probably your stress levels were a lot lower.

In the second example you were probably doing what came naturally to you and the stress you experienced was of the healthy kind. Lack of flow can occur for two reasons. Firstly if you've chosen a path that is clearly not right for you, leading to disappointment and stress, but also at the crucial time when you made a transition from one career to another – not realising that had you been given appropriate training and support you would have succeeded sooner.

At pivotal points in our lives, we make crucial life choices. For instance, the first time might be at school, perhaps when considering whether to go to university or take a gap year. Then as we grew older new challenges came along, i.e. whether to get married, making a major career change, moving house, or retiring. Some people make the right choice, with the right kind of support. Other people, however, make choices based on what they think they should be doing. For instance a student might want to attend drama school whereas their parents would prefer them to study medicine instead. The student may ignore their own instincts and follow their parents' advice. But in so doing might feel so unenthusiastic about their choice that they could eventually drop out of university later on.

Are you fulfilling someone else's expectations of you, rather than following your instincts and going after what you'd really love to do?

When you consider the career choices you've made throughout your life, where are you now? Do you think that work equals hard slog or are you enjoying your job so much that you don't actually feel like you're working at all?

On a scale of 1-10 rate how satisfying and rewarding your job is now. If it's less than 5, you may need to re-evaluate and make some changes. Because if you fall into the 'I loath my job' brigade, you may feel like a fish out of water, a square peg in a round hole, or just not in the groove!

Sometimes this lack of flow occurs for other reasons. Perhaps you've just been promoted but there are certain aspects of your new role that you're not prepared for, i.e. managing conflict, chairing meetings, strategic planning that kind of thing. You may not feel quite as confident as you did in your previous role, leading to a feeling of failure. But the only thing that could be standing in your way is lack of expertise in one specific area. That's it. But if you get into the habit of continually learning new things, and let go of having to know all the answers, the more successful (and more in the flow) you will be.

Perhaps you're facing redundancy and can't see a way forward. Are you prepared to keep learning and growing to create new opportunities for yourself? And don't overlook the transferable skills or skills you may have in other areas of your life which might open some doors for you and will keep the energy flowing in the right direction.

Like the two mice in the book, 'Who Moved My Cheese' who, instead of sitting around waiting to die of starvation because the cheese had ran out, put on their running shoes and went in search of more cheese (and new opportunities).

Robert T Kiyosaki author of "Rich Dad Poor Dad" says: *"Arrogant or critical people are often people with low self-esteem who are afraid of taking risks. You see if you learn something new, you are then required to make mistakes in order to fully understand what you have learned. There are so many 'intelligent' people who argue or defend when a new idea clashes with the way they think. In this case, their so-called 'intelligence' combined with 'arrogance' equals 'ignorance'."*

Some people reinvent themselves over and over in their search for the nirvana of the perfect career and aren't afraid to take a chance and try something new. I think the key here is first not to assume that what you are doing today is any reflection on what you could be doing tomorrow. Also be honest with yourself about what you're comfortable with, and be open to new ideas about what else you could try.

Which is where the next activity comes in.

HOW CAN YOU CHANGE IF YOU'VE BEEN IN THE SAME CAREER FOR YEARS?

Tom had been in the same role for a long time and it had become safe and boring. Being in a comfort zone was OK, but two things had started to happen to him. Firstly he had fallen behind as far as developing his skills were concerned. Secondly, he wasn't being stretched or challenged enough by having new things thrown at him. He was losing the edge. He was bored but also losing his confidence. However, facing change was making him feel very uncomfortable, even though he recognised that his career really wasn't taking him anywhere he wanted to go.

PERSONAL WORKSHOP ACTIVITY - BACK TO THE FUTURE

Take some time to think about moments in your life when you were really happy, where time stood still and you felt really confident and self-assured, and in 'the zone'.

- What were you doing?
- Which of those things do you no longer do?
- What changed?
- What stopped you from following your path to your destiny?

I was introduced to a very useful exercise in Fiona Parashar's book "The Balancing Act" which helps people

70

to reflect on their past (and therefore where they ultimately want to go) using a 'river of change'. This would appeal to you if you are a visual or a creative person, because it is a primarily a right brain activity. It doesn't require a great deal of thought but will help you gain perspective and look for trends and patterns in your life which could point to your future.

On a big piece of paper draw a river which represents the last 10 years of your life. Draw the river however you like, with whatever flow you like, and include anything or any person that you feel needs to be there. Fiona found that most people draw rapids, waterfalls, tributaries, bridges, people, rafts – it's up to you. Notice where the river is wide and flowing and where it narrows or dries up altogether. What recurring themes represent the good times? Where and how would you like the river to flow now? Now as you look back what lessons could you learn from this exercise?

WHAT DOES A DEGREE REALLY GET YOU?

A survey conducted by Monster.co.uk in 2008 found that 75% of people believe their career prospects have been unaffected by their academic results.

Universities and Colleges spend more time coaching students to pass exams than actually encouraging them to think, challenge, explore, to become curious and see the bigger picture.

Just one in ten who took the survey said they thought their qualifications and exam performance had played a key part in their job success.

The 'theory' of learning doesn't take into account that everyone is different, has their own contribution to make and a unique way of seeing things Doing some self development work is equally as important as passing an exam, in fact even more so, and will make you more employable.

The survey recommended pursuing extra-curricular activities that can be added to CVs to make candidates stand out. *"Work experience, summer employment and pursuing hobbies and extra-curricular activities will all help you to develop a broad range of skills that will ensure you succeed in your chosen career,"* it stated.

A recent survey by GRADdirect[2] found that 62% of employers believe transferable skills, such as communication and teamwork, are more important than academic qualifications.

"Why, anybody can have a brain. That's a very mediocre commodity. Every pusillanimous creature that crawls on the Earth or slinks through slimy seas has a brain. Back where I come from, we have universities, seats of great learning, where men go to become great thinkers. And when they come out, they think deep thoughts and with no more brains than you have. But they have one thing you haven't got: a diploma."
The Wizard of Oz

---

[2] Personnel Today 30 July 2008 *www.personneltoday.com/articles*

PERSONAL WORKSHOP ACTIVITY - SKILLS AUDIT

Take a look at the following six tables and tick your level
of skill in each category. This is a useful way to remove
any assumptions you have about what your level of skill
is now, what your strengths are, what skills you'd like to
develop and removes any potential roles that would be
entirely unsuitable for you.

Communication (Written & Verbal)		HIGH	LOW
	Drafting		
	Editing		
	Delegating		
	Listening		
	Mediating		
	Negotiating		
	Persuading		
	Presenting		
	Questioning		
	Reporting		
	Training		
	Writing		

Customer Service		HIGH	LOW
	Advising		
	Assisting		
	Caring		
	Coaching		
	Consulting		
	Co-ordinating		
	Handling Complaints		
	Selling		
	Supporting		

		HIGH	LOW
Cognitive/Analysis	Analysing Classifying Evaluating Generating Ideas Inventing Investigating Judging Learning Observing Problem Solving Researching Reviewing		

		HIGH	LOW
Numeracy Skills	Accounting Auditing Budgeting Calculating Checking Accuracy Compiling Statistics Estimating Measuring Recording Stock-taking		

Manual Skills		HIGH	LOW
	Constructing		
	Driving		
	Handling		
	Inspecting		
	Installing		
	Loading		
	Operating		
	Producing		
	Protecting		
	Repairing		

Leadership & Management		HIGH	LOW
	Appraising		
	Decision Making		
	Delegating		
	Talent Management		
	Interviewing		
	Managing Meetings		
	Market Awareness		
	Motivating		
	Project Management		
	Planning		
	Strategic Thinking		

If you have a burning desire to try something new then investigate how to narrow the skills gap and get some training. What hobby or interests do you currently have that you could combine together to turn into a new revenue stream for you? Learn and be inspired by other people who are already doing this.

Case Study: From Hairdresser to Polo Player

Ever heard the expression, 'If life gives you lemons, make lemonade'? Alex got himself a Saturday job at his uncle's hairdressing salon when he was 14. Alex didn't actually want to be a hairdresser, but he'd struggled at school because he is dyslexic, so he knew his options were limited. However, he wanted a job where he could meet lots of girls! He met plenty of them at the salon and eventually got himself a girlfriend, whose brother was a polo player.

Alex developed a passion for horses and playing polo which eventually more or less took over his whole life! He now plays polo as often as he can and owns his own Livery Stables which he rents out to a polo team. He took over the management of the hairdressing salon as well, which is now a thriving business. He loves his job, but his passion is polo and horses and he couldn't see himself doing anything else. He said to me that he is probably the only Polo Playing Hairdresser in the world!

If you find yourself in the position of having to make radical changes, but are open to the idea of diversifying then the following diagram may help you to see how this can be achieved.

If this was a mathematical equation it would look something like this:

Passion [Interest/Hobby/Talent] + Challenge [Adversity/Setback/Obstacle] X Attitude = Opportunity

So in Alex's case he was dyslexic so he couldn't pursue any further academic studies or career, therefore he had a challenge. He decided to try something else and with the right attitude he created an opportunity. He could have completely written himself off, or taken the easy way out, but he chose not to.

Case Study: Orthopaedic Nurse to Solicitor

Matthew started out his career as a nurse, working in a range of clinical areas. After being a nurse for 10 years he decided that it wasn't really for him, and went to college to study Business and Finance - a general qualification that enabled him to explore his strengths. It became apparent that he was actually really interested in law, and he went on to do a law degree.

After qualifying he got a job with a local law firm to complete his studies where he now specialises in wills, trusts, tax planning, estate administration (probate) and Court of Protection. His previous life as a nurse was not entirely wasted however because he brought with him some excellent transferable skills including patience, communication, listening, reassurance and discretion, all superb people skills very useful in his new role.

"If you don't design your own life plan, chances are you'll fall into someone else's plan. And guess what they have planned for you? Not much."

Jim Rohn, America's Foremost Business Philosopher

Here are some other career ideas:

- Travelling
- Voluntary Work
- Part-Time Work
- Vocational Courses
- Further Education
- Adult Education
- Social Enterprise

- Self Employment
- Joint Venture Partnerships
- Network Marketing
- Internet Marketing
- Home Based businesses
- Consultancy based on an existing skill

ACTION POINTS - CAPABILITIES

- What skills and capabilities do you already possess which need some improvement?

- What new skills would help you move forward?

- What skills need dusting off and looking at again?

- Who could support you in developing these skills?

- Take a long hard look and put this in your action plan.

Capabilities Power Question
Are you willing to go to any lengths
to achieve career satisfaction?
What's stopping you?

Louisa's train was still sitting at Aldgate East Station as she reached the end of this chapter. She had a nagging thought in the back of her mind that although the transition from being a graduate into a full-time job had been easy, she had under-estimated her level of skill as far as building her reputation and marketing herself within the organisation were concerned. She lacked confidence when communicating with others and her skills as far as asserting herself and building relationships needed some improvement.

She was well into her comfort zone on the hockey pitch however (if you could call running around in the mud comfortable of course), but in the office arena she was floundering. She felt isolated and quite vulnerable. She was hired, expected to carry out her role and get on with it.

Why did she have to learn through failing or falling flat on her face? This can't be the way to succeed surely? She decided that she would look on Amazon for some books on confidence building and pick a worthy person to model herself on by borrowing some of their attributes.

Tom looked around at the other commuters on the train with him. Half of them were asleep, several were talking and a few read a book or the newspaper. He didn't belong with this crowd he thought. He pondered on the times where he'd been at the crossroads in his career before and nearly jacked it all in, but lost his nerve at the last minute. "Could I honestly stand another 20 years of this? But what if I used a different strategy this time and went about things in a more structured way…? What skills do I ALREADY possess that I can take with me into a new career? Who do I need to become in order to make the leap?"

Just then an announcement was made to the passengers mentioning something about snow on the line up ahead. "Typical!" said Tom, so he went off in search of the buffet car to grab a coffee. It was going to be a long night, but plenty of time to reflect and start to make some plans.

"What's the name of this pub?" Dan asked the guy behind the bar. "The Emerald Inn," he replied.

Dan sent a text to his wife telling her where he was. That was a first! "I must be going soft," he thought. He got talking to the barman serving the drinks and discovered he used to be in the army but missed the camaraderie of being in the armed forces, so pub work suited him well. Then a profound thought struck Dan. "I'm a control freak!" He loved meeting new customers, being in the thick of it, but he'd been almost maniacal in his need to stay in control of everything. Consequently his business was like walking a pack of hungry hounds every morning and being dragged around the park at breakneck speed. Because of his background he hated failure, but was reluctant to ask for advice or support.

He sent another e-mail to his PA, "Get everyone in the office on Friday morning for a meeting – we're doing some planning," it said. "God what an idiot I've been."

In the next chapter we'll be taking a look at how your attitude and your behaviour shapes your success…

Principle 3 - Attitude

*"Just stay out of my Way! I'll get you
my pretty – and your little dog too!"*
The Wicked Witch of the West, The Wizard of Oz

DID YOU SLEEP IN THE KNIFE DRAWER LAST NIGHT?

I don't care what anyone says, you may have qualifications coming out of your ears, you may have 20 years' career experience behind you and an IQ of 160, but the fact remains that if you have unmet needs in your life these could impede your progress, even without you realising it. These might be completely subconscious drivers, simmering away beneath the surface. These could include a need for security, love, friendship, power or control for instance.

Now don't get me wrong, I'm not necessary just talking in the negative here. A need might include a strong creative streak, but your career might not provide any outlets for your creativity, leaving you feeling unfulfilled and bored. Maybe you have a very precise and ordered mind, but the environment you work in doesn't require those skills. You may be an absolute natural at entertaining and inspiring your customers, but instead you're stuck in the back office working on strategic planning and feel like a canary in a cage with it's wings clipped. If there is no outlet for your inherent talents you may have to comply and adapt in order to fit in. But that's like keeping the lid on a pressure cooker. I fell into this trap many times, trying REALLY hard to get things right, when I should have said to myself "look Wendy, stop and think. Is this where your talents are best spent?" I'd grown tired of working for someone who's keen eye for detail was driving me insane. And the harder I tried to be absolutely perfect the worse it got.

What I didn't know was that actually had I been a little more self-aware and made the conscious choice to apply my natural gifts and transition into something else, I would have found myself effortlessly moving into 'the zone'. I would have been less stressed and lacking in confidence, because once I'd identified something wasn't quite I could then proactively take action .

Which is why our emotions have a very important role to play here. Sometimes we may experience negative feelings and assume that these must be suppressed at all costs because we fear failure or being exposed as falling short in some areas.

Consequently our deepest needs stay buried for years, and our true potential never sees the light of day. But what if you were to stop for a minute and acknowledge an uncomfortable feeling as a sign or a warning flag that's madly waving at you which says: "hello, pay attention, we're trying to tell you something - you need to take some action here".

Interestingly if you were unable to feel any emotion this would seriously impact on your ability to make decisions, which is why emotions are crucial guides in our decision-making process.

At this point, if you are a man reading this, the subject of emotions and *feelings* might possibly be enough to bring you out in a rash or make you run for the hills. That's absolutely fine and I want to reassure you that this book isn't about getting in touch with your 'feminine side' or encouraging you to sit around in a circle singing sad songs with a tambourine. However, the word 'emotion' doesn't necessarily equate with weakness or failure. Emotions are warning lights for us to act upon. Feelings of slight unease could deteriorate into bigger and more profound emotions when these flags are ignored or dismissed altogether. But living with feelings of regret and guilt for instance, have so little energy attached to them they achieve precisely nothing.

So, if you bring your needs to work either because you aren't working to your strengths or haven't acknowledged that there's something amiss, then you might engineer situations in order to satisfy them and get a quick fix instead, which is a short term strategy. If your career doesn't provide you with an outlet for your natural talents and skills your progress up the ladder may be slow, especially if you either a) don't recognise there is a problem or b) aren't prepared to reflect on this or change direction to look for something more rewarding. The energy will have stalled and you won't be in the flow.

A need may become a blind spot that you don't even realise you have, although to other people it probably stands out a mile. This blind spot may manifest in any number of ways, to your detriment. For example, if you insist on your colleagues conforming to your methods (because your method works for you but not for them) others may resist you, argue with you, contradict you and then eventually fall out with you completely. For instance, if you're a big picture person but your superior is a lover of fine detail and they spent more time than is absolutely necessary pointing out the minor flaws in your plans, this may grate a little, leading to some frank exchanges and major differences of opinion. And who'd be right here? Is anyone ever absolutely right? We can be quite territorial when it comes to our needs and go to extreme lengths to preserve our 'patch' and may expect other people to conform or tow the line to preserve the status quo. I will explain a little later on why this is and what to do about that when I introduce you to the DISC behaviour system.

WHY DO NEEDS DRIVE US?

Imagine going out to buy a new car. When a particular model catches your eye what goes through you mind? It might not necessarily be: "that car has four wheels, an engine, five doors and central locking and loads of other features". At a deeper level you may sense only the status or power the car represents. Whatever button it pushes is unique to each of us.

You will be engaged with the buying process at an emotional level, which will influence your buying choice. This is sometimes referred to as emotional spending. Emotional spending works by stimulating the production of dopamine in your brain, which creates a temporary feeling of wellbeing. We may spend money to get a fix, which satisfies our innermost needs, but the feelings are only transitory.

So if you need status, power or attention for example, you will buy the car based on these needs, because needs are very strong drivers. I'm sure you've bought something that is way over your budget, because your heart was ruling your head and guess who won? Then you probably used logic to justify spending the money. This applies to new houses, hi-fi systems, shoes, BBQs, golf clubs, etc, and there are an infinite number of logical justifications for buying these things, but at the end of the day let's face it shopping is... seductive.

Kelvin Roberts, CEO Worldwide, Saatchi & Saatchi says: *"Erma Bombeck, the voice of the American housewife in the 1960s and 1970s, once said: 'the chances of going into a store for a loaf of bread and coming out with only a loaf of bread, are about 3 billion to one'. No one even bothers to go to the eclectic Colette store in Paris with a list. Colette seduces in the most French way: with personality and authentic charm. Customers love just falling into their arms."*

Some examples of needs include:

- Do you have to be right and find it hard to accept criticism?

- Do you like to win and to be in charge, even at the expense of other people?

- Is it important for you to be liked and make compromises in order to achieve this?

- Is security so important to you that you will resist change at all costs?

- Do you have an amazing talent for something that has no outlet and are trying to squeeze this into your career where it just won't fit?

- Are you being totally honest about what your needs are? What is your attitude to your career as a result?

Listen and pay attention to the signals you are receiving through your feelings and think about how you are currently dealing with them. Sometimes we deal with our needs in odd and not very logical ways. This is your subconscious mind, like a little kid brother or sister, desperately trying to make things right for you but without the benefit of experience or balanced rational thought.

ARE YOUR EMOTIONS RUNNING (AND RUINING) YOUR LIFE?

Emotions play a significant role in your career effectiveness and also your ability to handle stress. Your level of emotional intelligence will determine this. Therefore the person who really understands themselves, can successfully handle themselves in challenging situations, and at the same time bring the best out in others has a far higher chance of succeeding. In Daniel Goleman's book his research revealed that some people's emotions seem to be on a spectrum ranging from being extremely upbeat and optimistic at one end, to negative and melancholy on the other. He also found that this is linked to the relative activity of the right and left prefrontal lobes - the upper poles of the emotional brain.

According to Goleman: *"Research has revealed that people who have greater activity in the left frontal lobe, compared to the right, have a cheerful temperament; they typically take delight in people and in what life presents to them. They bounce back from disappointment very quickly.*

"Those with relatively greater activity on the right side of the brain are given to negativity and bad moods. They find setbacks hard to cope with, and they suffer because they worry all the time and feel depressed. In personality tests, those with marked right frontal activity showed distinctive patterns of negativity.

"In contrast, those with stronger left frontal activity saw the world very differently. Sociable and cheerful, they typically felt a sense of enjoyment, and were frequently in good moods, had a strong sense of self confidence, and felt rewardingly engaged in life."

Let's look at your behaviour and attitude. Does your response to certain situations mask an unmet need? Ask yourself what behaving in this particular way gives you? Could you do something more productive and positive instead which produces the same results?

For example, many times I've worked alongside people who've had a huge need to be seen as important. Deep down they yearned for more responsibility and authority, perhaps because their role didn't provide this for them. Therefore they deeply resented their colleagues being promoted or moving on.

Rather than doing something constructive about it their response was a pure knee-jerk reaction. They'd lead an avenging army to sabotage other people's success in an attempt to get their own needs met Did this make them popular? I don't think so. It was a short-term quick fix. This scenario repeated itself over and over in a destructive cycle and was very ineffective as a long-term strategy.

In 'The Celestine Prophecy' James Redfield said that The Sixth Insight tells us that we interfere with our evolution by getting stuck in trying to control energy by a process called a *control drama*. We literally stop the advancement of our destiny by using a repetitive childhood pattern of control, rather than allowing synchronicity to move us forward. He further goes onto say that, *"all dramas are covert strategies to get energy... covert manipulations for energy can't exist if you bring them into consciousness by pointing them out... the best truth about what's going on in a conversation always prevails. After that the person has to be more real and honest."*

> *"Perfectionism is the voice of the oppressor, the enemy of the people. It will keep you cramped and insane your whole life."*
> **Anne Lamott, Progressive Political Activist**

So when we're talking about needs it's very hard to ignore them because it's your feelings that drive you. If you recognise a recurring theme in some areas of your life then this may be because your instincts are trying to flag something up that requires your attention. Therefore, take charge and deal with your needs proactively.

If we, as human beings, are sometimes at the mercy of our emotions (whether we like it or even admit that) surely it is better to be consciously aware of these feelings and how our consequent behaviour affects those around us?

With conflict for instance, proactively preparing an adequate response results in less hurt feelings and a stronger relationship in the long term. This applies just as much to your performance at work as it does elsewhere.

In the meantime, do yourself a favour and get clear on your needs and what you really want. Develop the right attitude and focus on one big thing, one grand passion, adventure or challenge instead of focussing on the small things that don't make a difference. Successful people give their life focus, rather than grasping at straws in a desperate attempt to satisfy an unmet need.

MIND THE GAP

Picture the following scenario. A young man picks his girlfriend up in his new car to take her to the beach with the intention of asking her to marry him. She spends the entire journey going on and on about how she hates his new car and how could he even think of buying it. On and on she rants, behaving in a very petulant and childish manner. When they arrive at the beach, he stops the car, switches off the ignition, turns to her and says, "but that's not the surprise…"

If you're stuck in a frame of mind where you know you're not really handling something very well - mind the gap. Let me explain.

Regular commuters on the London Underground, will know that when a train arrives at the station, there is a gap between the train and the platform.

Just before the doors open, a voice on the PA system usually announces: "Mind the gap between the train and the platform as you leave the train". This gap is about 10 inches wide and we are warned to take care, so that we don't get a foot stuck or drop anything onto the track below. At nearly every station you hear this announcement and in some stations it's even written on the platform next to the thick yellow line painted on the platform. So at the point between alighting from the train and stepping onto the platform (or vice versa) you are warned to pay particular attention to what you are doing. You have to think about it. For a couple of seconds you are focussing your attention on, "oh, yes there's a gap, must be careful".

I use this analogy to bring your attention to the consequences of your behaviour. You have a choice as to your response in every situation. Because in most cases all you are doing is repeating a 'learned response'. For example going off in a huff, sulking, saying things like "you always do that", "why do you never listen?", "and remember the last time" or "whatever". However all behaviour can be unlearned and changed because it is essentially a choice.

JUST LET GO

To further elaborate on this point consider emotions as a spectrum. Take a look at the following diagram from The Sedona Method. This is an inner technique for 'letting go' that instantly puts you in touch with your natural successful self, so you feel confident, calm and in control in any situation. This spectrum illustrates how the words you use indicate where you are on this spectrum on a daily basis. Many people find that the reason they aren't moving forward is because they are 'holding onto' negative feelings, which is where The Sedona Method comes in.

APATHY	GRIEF	FEAR	LUST	ANGER	PRIDE	COURAGE	ACCEPTANCE	PEACE

The Sedona Method was originally developed by Lester Levenson. He was a physicist and successful entrepreneur, but in 1952 at the age of 42 he was very unhealthy and unhappy. He was depressed, had an enlarged liver, kidney stones, hyperacidity and stomach ulcers. Then he had a coronary. The stomach ulcers perforated his stomach and formed lesions. Later after his second coronary his doctors sent him home to die. But being a resourceful man, instead of taking his doctors' advice, he went into the laboratory of his own mind and found the ultimate tool for personal growth, which later became the Sedona Method – a way of letting go of all inner limitations. He essentially cured himself and not only that he found profound peace within which stayed with him until his death in 1994 at the age of 84!

The Sedona Method helps people who are holding onto 'stuff' they don't really need any more. It's this holding on which some people wrestle with (no pun intended). Even highly educated, intelligent people sometime struggle to see their way through to the other side of a problem. This includes feelings like inertia, procrastination, or even boredom. They hang onto them for dear life, because they can't see any alternatives. Their minds are closed to any options so the negative stuff takes up residence in their mind and, like an unwelcome lodger, hangs around for far too long.

The Sedona Method helps you to see how the words you use and the thoughts you hold in your mind are a reflection of your innermost feelings. However, when you live an abundant and full life of conscious choice, you will naturally gravitate further up this spectrum away from apathy towards acceptance and peace. This is indicated by the words and phrases you use on a daily basis. As an example, a happy and fulfilled person's conversation will be entirely different from someone feeling stuck, fearful and anxious. But here's my point, you choose those words. Nobody makes that choice for you.

Low self-esteem, boredom and lack of motivation could indicate a complete lack of joy and curiosity about life, brought about by holding onto feelings about people or experiences, which if not checked could go on for years and become a habit. And strangely some people are willing to go to any length to hold onto something, even to their own detriment. If you were to add up the number of hours a day you are feeling like that, ask yourself is it worth it? What does that ultimately achieve?

Consciously getting yourself into an upbeat and curious state of mind requires taking responsibility for your own well being, making a choice and taking action.

Changing your approach and your perception of a situation, is infinitely more energising don't you think than sitting around and playing the same scratched record of negativity and hopelessness over and over?

In Apathy, we see only the failure and limited resources available to us leaving us completely powerless.

In Grief, we are consumed with our negative feelings and look to others to help us. We do not yet have the wherewithal to make any effective change ourselves. The solution lies outside of us.

In Fear, our pictures are about doom and gloom, and we have a very pessimistic view of the world. We're more motivated than in grief, however our primary concern is self-protection.

In Lust, this is about wanting and a desire for things we don't have. Our feelings can be very intense. We are never satisfied and rarely enjoy life as it is, we just want more.

In Anger, we have more energy and have moved on, although this is all about getting even and making others pay. This can be self-destructive, obsessive and explosive, and could hurt others.

In Pride, we are still self-involved and we are full of nagging doubts. We are unwilling to change or move, and could be rigid and want to maintain the status quo.

In Courageousness, we have the willingness to move on without hesitation. Our thoughts and feelings are more positive and hopeful, we are more self-motivated and self-reliant. This has energy to it. It's the 'can do' thought process.

In Acceptance, we are quietly content and have no need to change anything, as we are more joyous and relaxed. We have even more energy available to us and our minds are full of more buoyant thoughts. We are enjoying life.

In Peace, we think, "I am whole". We are total and complete and our energy is quiet and calm. Our mind is clear, all is well and everything is perfect.

I encourage my clients to move along this spectrum, which has Apathy at its lowest point, moving up to the ultimate state of mind - Peace. I encourage them to write down the words that they routinely use every day, words that they may use out of habit, and start to replace these negative unsupportive words with positive affirming words and phrases. For example

"I'm never going to get over this," can be replaced with, "I will find a way" or "I am discovering new solutions all the time". Words have so much power. So 'watch your language'.

PERSONAL WORKSHOP ACTIVITY - EMOTIONS

Look at the spectrum of emotions and place a mark where you think you are at this moment on your journey.

Sit and look at the spectrum and ask yourself "what am I feeling?" Choose five or six words that describe how you feel and write them down. So for instance, lethargic, demotivated and sad, would be placed nearer the beginning of the spectrum than if you were experiencing elation, excitement and energy which would be more akin to courageousness. As I write this I am feeling focussed, energised and determined. So you could say looking at the spectrum I would put myself somewhere between Pride and Courageousness. Whereas feeling lethargic would place me under Apathy. Doing this exercise places conscious awareness on where you are on this spectrum.

The Sedona method encourages you to be as open as you can and lead as best you can with your heart and not your head. The first step to letting go of negative feelings is to name them, write them down and then start the process of neutralising their impact.

More information on the Sedona Method can be found on *www.sedona.com*

IF I ONLY HAD A BRAIN

In everyone's life we experience sudden events which we have absolutely no control over or couldn't predict, like fire, flood, earthquakes, that kind of this. However, there are other unfortunate things that happen to us which we might have a hand in. For example things like leaving your coat on the train, accidentally spilling a cup of coffee over important documents, taking 100 photocopies of the wrong paperwork, daydreaming in a meeting or inadvertently sending a stroppy e-mail and then regretting it later when it's too late, or being late for your own wedding.

We could define ourselves by one tiny mistake or allow the error to stay with us for days and cloud our thinking forever after we've said the 'F' word a few hundred times. For those moments when everything goes really dark and you're cursing in your best Anglo-Saxon, here are 9 ways to handle yourself. Yes, I did say that. Remember, in the realm of Emotional Intelligence, it's how you handle the situation and - more importantly - your response, which is key:

1. When you know you're not handling something very well, and have 'gone into one' at an inappropriate moment, stand aside – yes, take a physical step to the left and look at the space where you were standing. Instead of saying, "Doh! I'm such an idiot!" say to yourself: "Oh dear, aren't we going a bit over the top today? There I go again." Or just say to yourself "Cancel. Cancel. Cancel!" Just being aware is all that might be needed to help you gather yourself and calm down.

2. Before pushing the panic button or over-reacting: pause, think and take a breath.

3. Pause and think through what you are going to do or say next -compose yourself and think, "mind the gap".

4. Who do you trust so implicitly that you could confess all to, without feeling that they will beat you

up about it? (You'll already be doing a good job of beating yourself up anyway). Everyone needs a wise sage in their lives at moments like this.

5.   What positives could you take from the experience? For example what would you do next time, what else could you try?

6.   Remember, in any encounter you are always 51% responsible - so before lashing out take responsibility for your contribution in any encounter.

7.   Talk to yourself in a calming voice – you know, in a sort of Joanna Lumley kind of way, and just give yourself a break. Nobody's perfect.

8.   Holding onto negative feelings doesn't actually solve anything. Do this exercise. Get hold of a pencil. Now hold your arm out in front of you and grip the pencil really, really hard. How long do you think you could hold the pencil before your hand and arm starts to hurt? Eventually it will, won't it? Keep gripping the pencil for about 5 minutes. Now, just let it go. Let it drop to the floor. Feels better doesn't it?

9.   Accept that failure is actually the flipside of success and that all we're really doing anyway is failing our way to the top. So get over it and move on.

Case Study: When You
Think You've Lost Everything

Simon worked as a Senior Manager for a transport firm in London. His job was well paid with very good prospects. He was a very self-assured man with a great personality and an excellent future ahead of him. All lovely and marvellous you'd think.

On the strength of this he bought himself a 4-bedroom detached house and everything was rosy. Until one day everything started to fall apart. Another member of staff began to harass and bully him, but when he confronted the bully things got even worse and unbelievably Simon got fired! Then even when he took the case to an industrial tribunal he lost the case. Astonishingly his mother, who attended the tribunal every day, noticed that one of the panel members spent most of the tribunal asleep and only woke up just in time to agree with everything the judge said!

Because Simon couldn't obtain a reference from his previous employers he found it hard to secure alternative employment. So he retrained and obtained an HGV licence and did some long distance lorry driving for a few months instead. However, he could no longer afford the mortgage on his house so decided to rent it out. His tenants turned out to be extremely unreliable ne'er-do-wells. So in the end his mother suggested that he cut his losses, sell the house and move in with her, until he got himself sorted out.

Now, this was a massive blow to his ego, a grown man of 35 having to move back in with his mummy! He absolutely hated it. Then his girlfriend dumped him because he was slipping into a depression. Things were looking really bleak.

But one day he took some action, made a decision and announced to his mum, "I'm going away." He'd decided to book a flight to Spain, although he didn't exactly know what he was going to do when he got there. His mother left him at Stansted airport and as he went through the departure gate he turned to her and said, "Sorry mum, but I hope the plane crashes". He was so desperate he really didn't know what else to do and frankly he was past caring.

Fortunately, when he arrived in Spain he immediately secured a job as a Holiday Rep in a Hotel, where he met Anastasia who was a student research scientist. They formed a friendship and at the end of the season they remained in touch. Their friendship blossomed and they eventually got married. They now have successful careers and are blissfully happy living in the United States.

In these circumstances sometimes having the courage to take massive action can lead to change of the most remarkable kind.

WHAT PLANET ARE YOU ON?

Have you ever thought to yourself: "I should be like this", "Why aren't I more like her?", "Why can't I do that?", "Why is he/she soooooo annoying?"

In my past life as a rounders coach/team captain, one of the things I said to my team on the day of the match was to completely ignore what all the other teams were up to. Even if someone came up to me and said, "ooooh, watch them they have a really good team" or "don't worry about the opposition they're rubbish". If I listened to everyone it would either make me think that my team were finished before we'd even started or it would be a walk in the park. This in the end would affect our performance, our motivation and attitude.

What I was interested in was what we were doing.

This is an important point to make because if you spend too much time analysing the opposition, whilst at the same time not valuing your own skills, you are in essence taking most of your power away. But if you knew what your inherent strengths were, wouldn't it make life so much easier? If you knew why you felt very confident in some situations whereas in another context you felt totally the opposite, would that be useful for you? Knowing where to apply your strengths instead of putting yourself into situations that weakened your position has to be of benefit surely? For instance, when you work with a sports team, you always put your players where they are most comfortable, and therefore where they will excel. I was hopeless at bowling or being a deep fielder, but loved being back-stop which is where my strengths lay. Do you get what I'm driving at?

I discovered what the answer is through DISC Behaviour Assessments. This is a tool to help individuals raise their self-awareness so they work to their strengths and aren't spending 90% of their time desperately wishing they were someone else. Behaviour assessments identify our response to change, how we handle challenge, how we respond to rules and regulations and how we influence others.

The DISC Personality System is known as the universal language of behaviour and has its roots in the 'I Ching' or otherwise known as 'The Book of Changes'. This book was written over 3,000 years ago in China and essentially covers divination, man's relationship with the cosmos, and the universal order of things. It has links to Feng

Shui (e.g. Yin and Yang - light and dark, masculine/feminine, positive and negative). For every action there is a reaction. For us to succeed we must align ourselves with our core strength to enable us to be in 'the flow'. When we are in the flow we are more confident, energised and happier, thereby attracting the right people and opportunities to us.

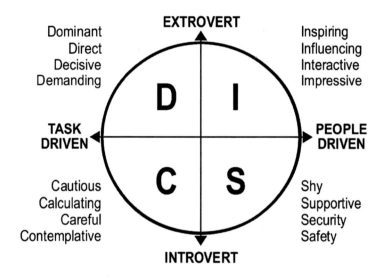

Research has shown that behavioural characteristics can be grouped into four major divisions, called personality styles. The acronym DISC stands for the four personality styles.

To illustrate this point if these core styles were planets they'd be something like this...

D   -   Planet Dynamo

I   -   Planet Influence

S   -   Planet Support

C   -   Planet Calculator

Dynamos - General Characteristics

Direct. Decisive. High Ego Strength. Problem Solver. Risk Taker. Self Starter.

These people are the doers, the pioneers, the leaders, they get things done. The downside to their character is that they may be a little insensitive to the needs of other people on their way to the top, because of their focus on getting the job done.

Recommendations: Give Dynamos something to focus on, a leadership role and a challenge. They want to do things "My way".

Dan Burnside exhibits many characteristics of a Dynamo. He may tend to take on too many projects, is reluctant to delegate and sets such a relentless pace for himself and others that he could eventually burn out.

Influencers - General Characteristics

Enthusiastic. Trusting. Optimistic. Persuasive. Talkative. Impulsive. Emotional.

These characters are great communicators and salesmen and women, they are very inspirational and wonderfully supportive and fun to be around. Unfortunately paperwork and routine really bore them so they might overlook important details because they might find paperwork and admin a bit dreary.

Recommendation: Influencers thrive in a people centred role where they have some influence, they love an audience. They want to do things the "Fun way".

Dan Burnside also exhibits some characteristics of an Influencer. He charges off in search of new opportunities and new experiences and finds getting to grips with the nitty gritty of admin and paperwork really tiresome and irksome. He would need the help of both a Supporter and a Calculator to help him take control and get a grip on his schedule and priorities.

Supporters - General Characteristics
Good listener. Team player. Possessive. Steady. Predictable. Understanding. Friendly.

Supporters are the solid, dependable people that keep the office going, are great listeners and really practical and reliable. This core type may find it difficult to accept change because they may see this as a threat.

Recommendations: Introduce change sensitively to these types and give them time to respond and to think things through in their own time. They prefer to do things the "Safe way".

Tom Tindall-Heart has some characteristics of a Supporter. Although steady and reliable, he is resisting change and is imprisoned in his own comfort zone. Over time it has become harder and harder for him to contemplate changing this job, but at the same time he feels that life is passing him by. He could learn a lot from the daring Dan by being more decisive and taking some risks because by playing it safe, he is missing out on opportunities and stagnating.

Calculators - General Characteristics

Accurate. Analytical. Conscientious. Careful. Fact-finder. Precise. High standards. Systematic.

Super clever at compliance, these people will work tirelessly in the background for you making sure that every detail is taken care of. Trouble is they are happy working alone and might not make a good team player. Their strong need to be right may make them appear rigid and conformist.

Recommendations: Always ensure that you provide quality answers to Calculator's questions and take the time to present all the facts. Glossing over the details may worry them. They want to do things the "Right way".

Louisa exhibits characteristics of a Calculator. Although she is very thorough her skills haven't secured her a promotion. She also exhibits some characteristics of a Dynamo which exerts itself only when she is on the hockey pitch. She requires new skills more akin to an Influencer to become more confident in expressing herself more assertively.

BLIND SPOTS – HOW AM I DOING?

As I mentioned earlier in the book, a blind spot is something that other people will notice except you. For instance have you ever been to a party when someone had commandeered the karaoke machine, but they weren't able to sing a note in tune? There they were belting out a song, not realising that everyone else was willing them to get to the end as soon as possible. That's a blind spot.

I remember listening to an interview with William Shatner in which he talked about the research he did on his autobiography years after he played Captain Kirk in

Star Trek. He went round to interview the cast who worked with him on Star Trek and it was only then that he discovered how much they really disliked him. He had absolutely no idea!

Our behaviour has a profound impact on other people and DISC is an extremely straightforward system that quickly and clearly identifies behavioural traits. Because once again, in the realms of emotional intelligence it's how you are able to empathise, build relationships and influence others which marks you out as a successful person.

A person's core profile operates with differing levels of intensity, depending on the context or environment that a person finds themselves in. In some situations, an attribute may be a strength whereas in another context, this same attribute may work against them.

For instance, if your core profile was a High C (Calculator) and you were a health and safety representative in a Nuclear Power Station, your profile will show that you have a keen eye for detail, compliance and strict adherence to procedures – this would work well for you in the context of Health and Safety/Compliance. However, give the same position to someone else with a high I (Influencer) profile and this could result in the person not being as effective because they would be more interested in interacting with other people than ensuring compliance with the safety procedures. This person therefore might not be as effective in the role because they are operating outside their normal comfort zone.

Not only that, if this person is in the wrong role (but not really aware of it) and concerns were raised about their performance, they could become extremely territorial and possibly even a bit defensive about it. Let's face it, nobody likes to feel a failure.

This is what being in the flow is all about – not forcing yourself into a role you're not suited to, but stepping back and reflecting on what's right for you. Working within your comfort or ' comfortable' zone means you will be operating under a tolerable level of stress. If you've consciously chosen a path that you know suits you, you will be in control of your destiny.

Blind Spots can manifest in the following ways:

- Being overly concerned with the fine detail, and missing the bigger picture.
- Getting carried away by the bigger picture and overlooking the fine details.
- Stubbornly resisting change and resisting new opportunities.
- Being distracted and diverted by new things, rather than consolidating and strengthening your current position.
- Unreasonable adherence to processes and procedures and stifling innovation and change.
- Making unilateral decisions on behalf of others and assuming that's what they really want.

Behavioural differences can also occur within teams if a low level of understanding and appreciation exists between them. This is where conflict and misunderstandings (power struggles) may occur.

Understanding and acceptance are the key words here. If you understand what makes you tick and appreciate why others are the way they are through identifying their core needs and drivers based on their DISC profile, then a greater level of acceptance and harmony will exist between you. For example, you might think you're a very thorough person, but to someone else they might call this being pedantic. Perhaps you're very spontaneous, but to someone with a different profile, in their book that's just being irresponsible. Or you may see your self as responsible, but to those closest to you they may see this as being domineering. With DISC you can see that nobody is inherently 'better' than anyone else, we're just all different. It's really that simple (so get used to it!).

Case Study (DISC): The Dream Team

I was called in to help a team working on a project. During my initial assessment of them it became clear that this team were not all singing from the same song sheet. With each coaching session it became very clear that they really didn't understand or appreciate each other. Because there wasn't a very happy atmosphere in the office, staff were working at home instead and making massive assumptions about each other.

My job was to help them to understand, accept and then work with each other in a collaborative, rather than a competitive way. This competition was causing stress, ill feelings and low morale. I used DISC as a way of demonstrating to them that people think and behave in different ways. Once everyone understood and appreciated these differences and accepted each other, their relationships and therefore morale improved massively.

If you would like your own personalised DISC Behaviour Assessment, log onto my website at *www.resolutioncoaching.co.uk* to find out more.

Case Study: Heading for Burnout?

Carolyn couldn't understand why she was feeling tired all the time. She would push herself harder and harder at work, setting herself an endless list of tasks and responsibilities and then arrive home to yet more tasks. She'd lost contact with her best friends and her daughters said she wasn't fun any more.

Every few weeks she would run out of steam and crash out, feeling exhausted and emotional. And most of all, she'd lost touch with who she really was, but she wasn't consciously aware of it.

Having not tried coaching before her initial approach was to assume that her coach would wave a magic wand and get it all sorted. However, after a few months of self-discovery, introducing a few new strategies and a complete re-evaluation of her life, she is a completely revitalised person. She's rediscovered herself, set herself free to get into the flow and lead a more meaningful and enjoyable life.

She is now happier than she's ever been for years, has reconnected with her old friends and her daughters have a happier, more carefree mum back. Not only that, but she has balanced her life and work in a more realistic way. The benefits just keep revealing themselves to her – months after the coaching has finished. Each month she reports yet another amazing thing that has happened to her. She has now taken up a new hobby which has given her life balance and harmony.

Coaching has introduced dramatic changes into her life. In fact the last time we talked she says that her life before she discovered coaching was completely different, her life has changed that much, she is without exaggeration one big bundle of happiness!

You can achieve tons more by taking action on your own challenges, rather than focussing on how wrong everyone else is. Focussing on everyone else's shortcomings is a sign that you may need to look at your own shortcomings first.

BUT ISN'T BEING SUCCESSFUL ABOUT BEING HAPPY TOO?

Now, before we all start to take ourselves too seriously, I know that work shouldn't all be hard work of course, and if you aren't enjoying yourself then it really is time to take stock. I think the advent of political correctness and health and safety has removed a lot of spontaneity from our lives. Don't misunderstand me, I'm not necessarily advocating 7 hours a day of side-splitting humour at work (although that does sound very appealing).

The black humour associated with undertakers, the police and the emergency services is well known; which is one technique that helps them to cope with sometimes very traumatic incidents.

A good laugh can be beneficial for your health. In fact laughing for at least 15 minutes a day is as beneficial to your lungs as a jog around the park! It can break the ice and introduce a bit of perspective to potentially tense situations.

Carol Ryff, a psychology professor at the University of Wisconsin-Madison who has been studying whether or not high levels of psychological well-being benefit physical health, says: *"There is a science that is emerging that says a positive attitude isn't just a state of mind."* She adds: *"It also has linkages to what's going on in the brain and in the body."*

Ryff has shown that individuals with higher levels of well-being have lower cardiovascular risk, lower levels of stress hormones and lower levels of inflammation, which serves as a marker of the well-being of the immune system.

"The difference between getting somewhere and nowhere is the courage to make an early start. The fellow who sits still and does just what he is told will never be told to do big things."
Charles M Schwab, 1862-1939 Industrialist

ACTION POINTS - ATTITUDE

- Is your behaviour masking an unmet need?
- What needs are you bringing to work that aren't being dealt with?
- Where is this revealing cracks in your integrity and credibility?
- Take steps to get an honest appraisal of yourself by asking for feedback.
- Who could support you in adjusting your attitude?

Attitude Power Question
What are you like when you are at your best? And do you get to play that role often enough?

Dan reached for his drink as he sat in the pub. The snow was beginning to settle and as it did he started to make some notes. He began to see how everything he did, from his need for material success, being a super hero, earning lots of brownie points, and knocking himself out 24 hours a day, was really something to do with being a dyslexic dropout at school. He was completely over-compensating so needed to tone everything down a bit and work out a new strategy. By racing towards accomplishment at 100mph he was essentially treating his body like a joy rider who'd nicked a car – flat out and hang the consequences.

He reflected on what he'd actually achieved and realised that if he slowed down, just a tiny bit and looked at things from a distance that he could find a different level of achievement which had more resonance.

Louisa knew that she was very ordered and precise at work, but hadn't paid enough attention to developing her people skills. Thus her boss saw her as an easy target to push around, knowing that Louisa wasn't assertive enough. She knew it was time to work on building up her self-confidence. What she also needed to do was transfer some of the confidence she possessed on the hockey pitch and bring it into the office occasionally. She'd love to flatten the Wicked Witch of the West of course, but that might be going a bit too far. She needed to reach the middle ground between outright aggression and passive resistance. There must be someone she could model herself on?

The doors of the train whooshed open and the familiar pungent aroma of the underground wafted into the carriage. Where did that smell of tar mixed with cat's pee come from? She had another 15 stops to go before she arrived home. She sent her mum a text telling her she'd be late.

Tom watched as the train along with its 12 carriages snaked out of the station. It was dark outside, dark and forbidding. He reflected on how he saw his future approaching. He'd spent so long avoiding the inevitable that he was now trapped in a cosy but very uncomfortable prison. But the outside didn't look that inviting either.

He thought about his decision to give up horticulture and garden design 20 years ago. Who was he listening to back then? And why did he listen to them? And what did they know anyway? He made some notes in his Filofax, there must be an answer here! By tomorrow, his life would never be the same again, because it couldn't be as boring and tedious as it was right now.

So far we've looked at your environment, skills and attitude. I'm not saying that by the end of this book you'll be a black belt in personal development, but I hope few light bulbs will have been switched on already.

Principle 4 - Packaging

"Words and magic were in the beginning one and the same thing, and even today words retain much of their magical powers. By words one of us can give another the greatest happiness or bring about utter despair; by words the teacher imparts his knowledge to the student; by words the orator sweeps his audience with him and determines its judgments and decisions. Words call forth emotions and are universally the means by which we influence our fellow-creatures."
Sigmund Freud

ARE THEY BEING PROMOTED RIGHT OVER YOUR HEAD?

There was a time when I used to wonder how to bring people around to my way of thinking more quickly. I'd sit there desperate to point out my astute and incredibly incisive observations which everyone else had completely overlooked. This would happen time and time again. I'd sit there thinking, "I have a solution, but nobody's paying attention to me!" But I could never quite articulate my thoughts in a way that made any impact at all.

So I began to look more closely at this whole subject of persuasion, for example at networking, selling and presenting. In fact I realised that I had to re-evaluate the impact I was making on people. Eventually the penny dropped. The powerful cocktail that was required to "knock 'em dead" included the clothes that I was wearing, but also my use of language, and how I used my voice. Plus my confidence levels (or how I was feeling) were reflected in my body language, so I needed to at least look confident even if sometimes I didn't exactly feel like that.

As far as my voice was concerned, the only skill I possessed which was remotely connected to public speaking, was my experiences of singing in the school choir! But singing in a choir is a slightly different way of engaging your audience; in a choir it's a team effort so you're not necessarily in the spotlight.

My background as a PA meant that I was excellent at preparing the material (for other people), but not actually delivering it. My first attempts at public speaking weren't exactly a disaster, but there was room for improvement. So, I went on a mission to learn everything I could about public speaking and here are a few tips that have really made a big difference to me, which if you have something important to say, can help you too.

I've gradually amassed various skills which have made a massive difference to the way people treat and perceive me. I watched and learned, over and over and over.

Because it's the way your message is delivered which makes such a gigantic difference to how it is received. You only have to listen to George Clooney talking and you'll know exactly what I mean. He starts to speak and you are hooked. But that's not the entire picture.

It's a combination of how you look, how you feel, how you've prepared and the way your message is conveyed. Communication is an art form which combines to influence how your audience receives your message. Of course the path to developing your skills involves a certain element of risk; the risk of making a fool of yourself or putting yourself in the firing line. I was willing to do this, because the only other option open to me was to do nothing and stay exactly where I was and not be taken seriously.

I love good storytellers who use their voice like a musical instrument. They know all about contrast, pitch, tone and warmth. It's no accident that the French and Italians are perceived as so attractive and seductive. Wouldn't you agree that even hearing something as mundane as a train timetable read by a Frenchman is so much more enticing? Frankly, you hear the voice and you're done thinking. Instead, you're probably not even listening to the words they are saying. Their charming voice has disarmed you, and thus you've become a friendly audience for them – giving them a chance to be heard and understood more quickly.

Communication, both verbal and non verbal, can be learned just like any other skill.

Let's use music as an example. I took up the cello at the age of 11 and worked my way up to Grade 7 by the time I was 21. Of course mastering all the techniques to become a great cellist takes time and I am far from that. However as my technique grew my ability to sway my audience intensified. Sitting amongst the cello section of a

Symphony Orchestra comprising 8 cellos all playing in harmony with each other is possibly one of the most blissful experiences I have ever had. And if that isn't transferred to the audience in a very intense way, I'd be very surprised.

And it's the same with human interaction. The combination of the clothes you wear, a compelling voice, the words you use and your body language are an intoxicating mix in the right hands. These elements say more about you than anything written on a piece of paper, a degree or in a CV.

I've sat in the audience listening to dreary presentations that did a better job than heavy-duty tranquillisers. The presenter missed a big opportunity to influence me, because I was more interested in the tea and biscuits than in anything they had to say.

"Our thinking creates problems that the same type of thinking will not solve."
Albert Einstein

Allow others to get a glimpse of your unique qualities and personality by firstly packaging yourself more attractively, so that your audience starts to care about what you're saying. People do judge a book by its cover and if you've packaged all the elements of yourself effectively your presentation or the key interview will get the reception you desire.

WHAT DO OTHERS SEE OR HEAR FIRST WHEN THEY MEET YOU?

The tonal quality, volume and the pitch of your voice are seriously underestimated when attempting to persuade others. Your voice has such a fundamental impact on others, more so than the words you actually say! Research has proven that if your voice is clear, well modulated and pleasant on the ear, people will assume that you are in fact more intelligent than you actually are! People will be drawn to you like bees are to honey!

"Also crucial can be your personal appearance, your language and patterns of speech, your personality and demeanour, and your general level of professional courtesy. Anything that affects the way you look and sound to the customer can affect your level of believability."

Robert B Miller and Stephen E Heiman with Tad Tuleja,
"The New Conceptual Selling"

HOW I TURNED MYSELF INTO A COMPETENT PUBLIC SPEAKER

What follows are some hidden secrets that I developed on the road to learning public speaking.

6 POWER SECRETS TO DEVELOP YOUR VOICE

1. Locate Your Voice

I credit Richard Bandler, the founder of NLP, for the following exercise. It helps you to locate where in your body your voice is resonating so that you notice the difference.

- Stand up and touch your forehead and at the same time say, "This is my voice."
- Then touch your nose and repeat the phrase again.
- Then touch your mouth and repeat the words.
- Touch your throat and repeat, touch your chest and repeat.
- Then touch your diaphragm and repeat.

Notice how the pitch of your voice gets deeper as you focus on different parts of your body. The higher in your head your focus is, the higher your voice is, and it will be less effective. Did you notice the difference? Richard encourages everyone to practise bathing people in tonality. Good tonality is incredibly powerful. High-pitched squeaky tonality doesn't have the same impact as a rich voice, which reminds you of a warm cup of coffee, does it?

2. Round Your Vowels

Jonathan Altfeld suggests that you stretch out the round vowel sounds, in his Irresistible Voice CD's. Rich, warm, rounded vowel sounds have a more appealing tonal quality than short, harsh staccato sounds. Again recall how the French use language. Listen to how musical and lyrical their language is. It is also so appealing because they use soft consonants. A voice with very stark, hard consonants is not as compelling as words spoken using nicely rounded vowel sounds, with soft consonants.

3. Vary Tone, Pitch, Speed & Volume

Treat your voice like a musical instrument by dynamically varying the tone, speed, pitch and volume, and varying your facial expression. For example you can achieve this by showing enthusiasm when you talk to people, and placing e m p h a s i s on some words by using appropriate gestures. Pause between sentences, and take a deep breath before continuing to speak. Squeeze emotion out of words by talking from your heart not your head. We love to hear stories not just loads of facts.

4. Breathe From Your Diaphragm

Remember to breathe properly from your diaphragm. Trained singers use this technique. Speaking from your throat and keeping the air stuck there turns your vocal chords into a restrictive tube, which is fine if you want to sound like Donald Duck or Mr Bean, but not if you're after some serious funding or a promotion.

Take a deep breath from your diaphragm, open the airway and allow the air to push out through your mouth while speaking. This will produce a more resonant quality to your voice. Plus if your voice is emanating from your throat you will have to work harder to project it to the back of the room and the back row! Also, be careful if you talk too quickly or tend to look down when you speak. Talk to the back wall if you have to, if you feel uncomfortable with making eye contact (although making and keeping eye contact for a few seconds is recommended). Use the same technique even if you are in a small room.

5. Hold More Air

Practise holding more air in your chest. This gives your lungs greater capacity and therefore strengthens your voice. Lie flat on the floor, take a deep breath and then slowly breathe out. At the same time, count 1,2,3,4, etc. The more numbers you can speak without running out of breath the better your lung capacity is and therefore your ability to project your voice into a room to have more impact. You should aim for a count of 40 or more.

6. Watch Your Intonation

Richard Bandler explains how this works in his book "Persuasion Engineering". The pitch of your voice will determine how a sentence is received. If the pitch rises at the end of a sentence it is 'heard' as a question. If the pitch remains the same at the end of the sentence it is heard as a statement. If the pitch drops at the end of the sentence this is received as a command. A pitch drop at the end of a sentence opens the 'command module of the mind', i.e. the person on the receiving end registers this and will have no alternative but to obey you... This skill is particularly important if you are a woman because if all your sentences rise in intonation at the end then your message will be received as a question, which gives the other person the option to say no to you.

Let me show you. Take the sentence "Would you like fries with that?" This could be said in the following three ways...

The voice rises in intonation at the end of the sentence.

The voice is neutral and doesn't change intonation one way or the other. This is known as 'charge neutral'.

As a STATEMENT sentence.

The intonation drops at the end of the sentence, which opens the command module of the mind and has much more power! It is here you can ask for the earth, and get it.

Go to *www.altfeld.com/mastery* for more information about using your voice. Jonathan Altfeld has years of experience in this field and has developed exercises designed to help you get the most from your voice to help you become more dynamic and appealing.

PERSONAL WORKSHOP ACTIVITY
– THOUGHTS BECOME THINGS

Visualise the people you know whom you automatically warm to. You don't often hear them talking about death, destruction and the dreadful weather. It's the person who's good to be around who makes everyone around them feel great that you will be irresistibly drawn towards. Therefore notice what happens to the people around you when you speak in positive and upbeat terms.

One very important point here is this: Thoughts Become Things. What you think about comes about – eventually. Put energising thoughts, upbeat words and encouraging vibrations into the universe and you'll get more of the good stuff back. So the next time you meet anyone whether it's at a party, a networking event, or on a bus, you never know where that conversation may lead or who they know, so watch your language.

"From now on, as you hear yourself disastrously blaming justifying, or complaining, cease and desist immediately. Remind yourself that you are creating your life and that at every moment you will be attracting either success or crap into your life. It is imperative you choose your thoughts and words wisely!"
T Harvey Eker, 'The Secrets of The Millionaire Mind'

IT'S THE WAY I TELL 'EM!

Do you have friends who have a knack of telling jokes? It's interesting how the same joke told by two different people, will get a different response, even though it's exactly the same words told in more or less the same order.

Over the years I realised what an incredibly powerful role words play, in the right hands. You can change someone's state of mind with words. You can help someone change their perception of a challenge. Words used skilfully can provide options and new ways of tackling the same problem. Structuring your language positively and re-framing key statements plays a pivotal role here. When applying this to your career path the relationship you develop with words and how you apply this skill with using them can make you more persuasive and therefore more successful.

How you articulate your message is critical because it's the way that message is received by another person that will determine how they respond to you. Therefore, your message has to be transmitted in the right way in order for it to be beneficially received and acted upon. Remember this key point: in any interaction you are always 51% responsible. Which means that if someone doesn't 'get' what you're trying to tell them ask yourself, "is it the transmitter or the receiver that's at fault?" Are you both tuned into the same radio frequency? Are you trying to transmit Radio 3 when they're receiving Radio 1?

10 TOP TIPS FOR GREAT COMMUNICATORS

1. Listening

Whether you are in sales, lead a team or need to build strong relationships with your colleagues, one of the most important skills you need to learn is to actually say nothing at all. In other words, listening. Remain silent when the other person is speaking and do not interrupt.

There are 3 different levels of listening. Level 1 is surface listening that we all do when we've got half our attention on the telly or our computer at the same time as talking to our partner or friend for instance.

Level 2 is where we give the other person our full attention but we're still thinking our own thoughts or are trying to think up something witty to say in return, perhaps to impress them.

Level 3 is where active and reflective listening takes place. This is serious listening. Here you give the other person your absolute undivided attention by maintaining eye contact and really 'hearing' what they are saying. The other person will feel appreciated and validated and it's very flattering. And frankly when you're in their presence it's like being plugged into the national grid – totally riveting.

Demonstrate reflective listening by giving the other person plenty of space to tell their story. Acknowledge that you are listening to them through your gestures and with encouraging comments, for example, "Yes, go on..." Most people really love being listened to at this level, it's a whole different experience. By actively working on this skill your status in their eyes will be elevated considerably.

2. Reflect their words

If you are in a situation where another person is feeling particularly upset and needs to feel understood, then use their words. Reflect their words back to them and match their level of energy. If someone says, "I feel undervalued", rather than saying "So, you feel that we don't appreciate you?" instead say, "What makes you feel undervalued?"

When I used to work in car insurance we'd occasionally get customers calling the Branch Manager to complain. I would let them rant on to get everything off their chest for about 5 minutes. Then I would respond, using their same level of energy and simply say "Yes, that's dreadful! I totally agree with you, we must get this sorted out immediately!" Just hearing that I empathised with their anger really calmed them down.

I've heard stories of people calling a business to obtain recompense on a problem and the customer service representative on the other end of the phone spoke to them like they were holding a counselling session which was completely counter-productive, and guaranteed to make the customer spontaneously combust rather than reach any common ground. By being too calming and detached they made the caller feel that they weren't being understood.

So with conflict get as close as you can to the other person's view of the world by using the words and mirror the feelings that the person you are speaking to relates to. When you reflect back to them using your own language you've demonstrated that you can't empathise with them and reaching a closer understanding will be lost.

Additionally if you're meeting someone face to face to solve a problem, if you both stand (or sit) facing in the same direction, this creates a collaborative relationship where both parties can work towards finding a solution together and therefore is beneficial to both sides. In certain circles, that's known as a win-win.

3. It's Not About You

People love talking about themselves. Sure, some people when asked will talk for hours about themselves without ever reciprocating or even pausing for breath and of course there's no guarantee that you will still be awake! An ideal example would be like a game of tennis, you lob over a question, they respond with a reply. So you serve a new question and they come back with a comment and so on. So, when meeting new people be interested rather than interesting. Let the other person talk and ask them some questions. It's the answers that you receive which will provide you with an opportunity to comment specifically on something they've said. For example, "oh yes I have the same car" or "I went to the same university" or "I love fishing too" – these commonalities build trust and therefore pave the way for forging a new relationship.

"I look at the depth of people's lives, rather than just what you've done in business," says Allen Shardelow of Heidrick & Struggles, Executive Search. *"I want to know about the soft issues: who you are, where you were born, where you grew up, what kind of memories you have of your childhood, whether you still have friendships with the people you grew up with…"*

This kind of background can be deeply significant, Shardelow says, *"For instance, if you need to be in a relationship-type role, which most executives do, but you're not good in relationships, I would be sceptical."*

4. Don't Ask Why

When in a challenging situation, say for example dealing with a partner or colleague who may be feeling upset or stressed, here's a really big clue to getting through to the other side. Be careful when asking a 'Why?" question. The word why puts people on the defensive and should only be used sparingly and when you feel it is comfortable to do so. A "Why?" question makes the other person feel that they have to explain, or give a correct answer. It gives no room to explore possibilities so should be used with caution. The quickest way to end a conversation or to get someone running for cover is to ask "why?"

5. Be Creative

When trying to find solutions or exploring possibilities, use "what", "how", "where", "who" or "when" questions. For instance, if you have someone on your team who isn't performing very well, rather than saying, "why did you do that?" to which they may be forced to either lie or avoid the issue, ask, "So, what do you think?" That feels so much more supportive doesn't it? This also works well in a sales environment. Asking 'open' questions like this initiates conversation and exploration rather than closing down the other person's options.

6. Draw A Picture

If you lack confidence in being able to convey your message clearly in meetings or if someone doesn't understand what you are telling them, use a metaphor or draw a picture. Some people are very visual and respond better to information conveyed to them using different mediums. Draw a picture on a scrap of paper rather than give a lengthy explanation. It gets the message across more directly and works for individuals who may be overloaded by lengthy explanations or too many words. Be creative.

"If people are coming to work excited, if they're making mistakes freely and fearlessly, if they're having fun, if they're concentrating doing things, rather than preparing reports and going to meetings - then somewhere you have leaders."

Robert Townsend, Professor of Economics in the Department of Economics at MIT

7. Be Yourself

People like to work with and buy from people they like, know and trust. So be yourself right from the start. Most people can spot a phoney very quickly anyway and know when the other person isn't being genuine. Openly talk about who you are and share your ideas and feelings. This gives the other person the opportunity to discover if you have any common interests between you which is the first step in building trust and stronger relationships.

8. Always Assume You're Assuming

Occasionally we make judgements about other people which may be incorrect. If you judge someone you've only just met based on an assumption i.e. because of their appearance, and you don't like what you see, your behaviour towards them could be affected. So before you judge others assume you're assuming and consciously put your assumption aside. Then take the time to get to know the person at another level, regardless of the fact that they may have unusual features or strange hair. You may well come to the same conclusion you had at the beginning; but then again you may not and it could be the start of a beautiful friendship.

9. Be Generous In Your Praise

When giving feedback, use an NLP technique called the 'Feedback Sandwich'. The Feedback Sandwich goes like this: Firstly state specifically what did go well and what you liked. This is the first slice of the feedback. The bad news will be sandwiched between two pieces of good news. So you then tell them what didn't work well. Complete the sandwich with what you would like them to do better next time, or how they could improve. For instance:

Example: "This chicken tastes good but it's a bit spicy…" The statement following "but" negates the statement before "but". So the real meaning received by the cook is "The chicken is not good."

This statement could be improved with:

"This chicken is spicy but it tastes good…" The cook is focused on the chicken tasting good with some helpful input into making it taste even better next time by adding less spice.

Most people will usually remember the last piece of information given to them so by making this last message upbeat you will keep them motivated and happy.

10. Sensory Feedback

Sensory feedback makes a big impact on the person you are delivering it to. There are three ways to communicate feedback and appreciation using sensory awareness. Most people fall into 3 sensory categories: visual, kinaesthetic or auditory. Visual people translate and understand information received through what they see. The kinaesthetic people, are more 'touchy feely' and the auditory people are highly tuned into what they hear. If you are curious to know how to work out the difference just ask your staff or colleagues to tell you about their last holiday. Depending on which category they fit into, they will say something like this:

Auditory
- I loved hearing the sound of the sea
- The music sounded wonderful
- The silence was fabulous

Kinaesthetic
- The weather was really warm
- I felt just right at home
- Everyone was so welcoming

Visual
- The scenery was amazing
- The villa was beautiful
- The sky was so blue

The auditory person may talk quickly and have a lot to say for themselves. The kinaesthetic person will talk more slowly, because they run things past their feelings first and let things sink in, so they may appear more thoughtful. The visual people will notice things about you, for example if you've got new shoes on and are more likely to remember what you were wearing last week.

When giving feedback visual people will appreciate a card, kinaesthetic people will appreciate something that makes them feel good, like a voucher for a spa treatment, whereas the auditory person will know they are really appreciated if you sit down and actually give them face to face feedback and are genuine about it. An e-mail just won't have the same impact.

It's also important to notice what your own primary sense is because what you appreciate may not be what other people appreciate. Of course you may be a combination of more than one of these three senses and may identify with all of them. I am an even split across all three. It is handy to be aware of this when resolving conflict because others will usually tell you what they want using their own language – i.e. "I hear what you are saying", "I feel there is something wrong" or "I see we have a problem here".

There are two other senses that I've not mentioned - taste and smell. If these are your primary senses then when talking about your holiday it's the aroma of food and flowers that may be at the front of your mind.

"The people who make a difference in your life aren't the ones with the most credentials, the most money or the most awards. They're the ones who care. If you want to be remembered for being important to someone's life, make them feel appreciated."

Jack Canfield, Success Coach and Author of Chicken Soup for the Soul

The Secret Power Of Words

Fall in love with words. Words persuade, compel, seduce, entertain and inspire. Words - and how they are spoken - have literally changed lives, won wars and swayed whole nations. Queen Elizabeth saw off the Spanish Armada with her rallying speech to the British Fleet. She capitalised on the power of words and used them to instil courage and inspire her subjects.

Be very mindful of the words that pepper your conversation. Do they uplift others or put others off?

For instance be careful with the use of buzzwords. Saying things like "yep, we're on message", "let's run this one up the flag pole" or "let's try some blue sky thinking" may sound impressive when in fact it might have the opposite effect and make you look, well I think you see what I'm saying here.

PERSONAL WORKSHOP ACTIVITY
- 50 THINGS I LIKE ABOUT ME

Some people find it a challenge to feel or see anything positive in anything or anyone around them. Over time they've programmed themselves to only pay attention to the negatives and have turned away from positive messages. To 'reactivate' this part of their mind I ask my clients to write down 50 things that they like about themselves, record their achievements or remember what other people have said about them that made them smile. In fact I get them to record on a daily basis anything at all that pleases them or makes them happy. From big achievements such as, "I won the Scholarship" to day-to-day observations such as, "I woke up today to the snow and it was so beautiful".

When we are children we are open and curious about life and love to be delighted, amused and entertained. We look forward to the arrival of Father Christmas, summer holidays, parties and our birthday. But sometimes life gets in the way and the joy we had in our hearts fades away. Thus some people find it harder and less 'realistic' to see the world in positive and upbeat terms. Until seeing the world as a dark and unforgiving place becomes a habit. It's easier to expect bad news, bad service, unreliable friends and disappointment, and to continually have low expectations of everything and everyone.

However, once they look around and are willing to see that there are plenty of things to be thankful and happy about their view of the world shifts quite radically.

I love to think of the universe as this big jolly fuzzy bear who's dozing in the corner waiting for instructions. He wants to please you with unexpected ice creams, crazy thunderstorms on a summer evening, a smile from a stranger and that pair of shoes in your size. All you have to do is ask, be grateful when your call is answered and to expect even more good things.

"Put 'em up, put 'em up! Which one of you first? I can fight you both together if you want. I can fight you with one paw tied behind my back. I can fight you standing on one foot. I can fight you with my eyes closed. Oh, pull an axe on me, eh? Sneaking up on me, eh? Why, I'll... Ruff!"
The Cowardly Lion, The Wizard of Oz

TURN OFF YOUR E-MAIL

There are some organisations that are encouraging their staff once a week to communicate with each other using any method they like except e-mail. Before the advent of e-mail people actually picked up the phone or walked around their desks to talk to each other. Funny, eh? Firms such as US Cellular and Deloitte and Touche have been experimenting with a different e-mail policy for some time.

The downside of an over-reliance on e-mail is that people are forgetting the subtle art of communication and becoming lazy. Plus there are numerous ways that one person could construe a message contained within an e-mail if it is grammatically incorrect and when you add this to a poor grasp of e-mail etiquette this could ruffle a few feathers. I am sure nearly everyone has used e-mail to vent their anger at a colleague instead of meeting them in person, only to regret it later. Sometimes there is a big temptation to include far too much information or to use CAPITAL LETTERS, which is the equivalent of SHOUTING!

The advantage of talking face-to-face means you are able to pick up the non-verbal cues which form an essential part of the communication process. You can't pick up these subtle cues in the written word. Poorly written e-mails could lead your colleagues to make assumptions about you that are completely incorrect. So today, just for a change, pick up the phone and talk to a human being.

BODY LANGUAGE

Your body language is that ever so clever communication tool which allows others to see what we're thinking and feeling. Being able to pick up these non-verbal cues is inherent in all of us. Generations and generations of prehistoric tribes made do with non-verbal means of communication — animal-like guttural sounds, gestures and drawings — to fulfil their requirements before they latched on to a language.

In addition the ability to read non-verbal cues is useful in building rapport. If you notice things like the sparkle in someone's eyes or nervous gestures for instance, even though these are instinctive observations, you are actually communicating at a very sophisticated level.

I remember wandering around a cathedral a while ago with my sisters. I was feeling really down about where my business was going and wanted some quiet time to soak up the atmosphere and generally get away from the hullabaloo. Unfortunately the curators who were there to take people on guided tours would not leave us alone. It was clear from our tone of voice and our body language that we just wanted to be left in peace, but they weren't

Principle 4 - Packaging

'tuned in' to what we were desperately trying to tell them through our body language, which was, "please go away!"

Therefore at some level our decisions are influenced not so much by what other people say but through the non-verbal cues that you pick up. This speaks to us at a very subtle but far more powerful level.

When you go for an interview it's important to realise what message you are conveying with your body language. For instance one boss that I used to work for was conducting some interviews and one particular candidate spent the whole interview sitting back in his chair with his hands behind his head. He was coming across as over-confident. Needless to say he didn't get the job.

Another boss I worked for would periodically hold interviews for new members of staff. The panel consisted of three interviewers. For a bit of fun the panel asked me to tell them at the end of each day which candidate I thought they had chosen. All I had to go on was the candidate's name, what they looked like and the very brief conversation I held with them when they arrived. 9 times out of 10 I always picked the person they hired. I don't think that I had any particular skill here; I just picked things up about their body language and their demeanour which wouldn't be evident in a CV. We can all do this but sometimes we ignore it in favour of the logical approach. I wasn't after winning any prizes for that observation by the way, although it does appear that women do have the edge over men in this area.

In a study conducted at the University of Pennsylvania Medical Center in 2004 90 percent of men and women correctly identified expressions of extreme sadness in pictures of womens' faces. When the researchers showed them a more subtly sad face the men's identification dropped to 40 percent but the women's stayed at 90. In other words, men seem to understand obvious emotions but more restrained cues can go right past them

"This implies different emotional-intelligence capabilities for women and men," says Louann Brizendine, M.D., a clinical professor of psychiatry at the University of California at San Francisco and the author of The Female Brain This may explain why women often find themselves crying to (or yelling at) their partners. *"It's an adaptive behaviour for females to cry in front of a male,"* says Brizendine, *"because he often doesn't get it until you're in tears."*

Body Language Tip - Having A Bad Day?

When you are having a bad day this will be reflected in your body language. However, you can make this work for you the other way round. For example, deliberately adopting a very positive stance will affect how you feel

Stand up with feet apart and arms at your sides. Now take a deep breath and look up at the ceiling or the sky. Lift your arms out to your sides, bringing them up palms upwards. Now breathe in and as you do that – smile. Doesn't that feel good? In essence what this demonstrates is that it is a two-way street. Your mind affects your body and your body affects your mind. By the way it's best not to do this exercise in the lift or on the underground.

PERSONAL WORKSHOP ACTIVITY - DRESS AS IF YOU MEAN IT

Think about what you are wearing. Are you dressing to create the right impression? You see, how you look affects the way other people perceive you. That first impression leaves an imprint on someone else's mind and they will be drawn towards or away from you because of how you make them feel and think.

That first impression is called the halo effect. Make a great impression on someone the first time you meet them and no matter how many times you stuff up later they will remember your first meeting and be beneficially inclined towards you.

In any situation it is vitally important to dress appropriately. For instance women assume they will have more impact if they wear a black suit, black shoes and a boring white shirt, when in fact wearing lighter colours makes you more approachable. On the other end of the spectrum wearing flip-flops won't create a professional image either, neither does using very strong perfume or wearing short skirts, plunging necklines or clunky jewellery.

If you are unsure quite what to wear at an interview for instance here are 7 top tips:

1. Try and find out before the interview if the company has a dress code.

2. Always dress UP for the job - it looks as though you care about the role and you are in a stronger position than if you dress down.

3. If you don't wear a suit try a neutral coloured jacket (black, grey or brown) over a smart blouse, top or shirt and tie. If you know colours that suit you - wear them.

4. Aim for a good fit when choosing the outfit - when your clothes fit well they become a natural extension of you and you forget about them.

5. Don't forget the importance of good grooming, hair, nails and polished shoes - they will be noticed. Don't hide behind long hair or facial hair.

6. Accessories can make or break an outfit, handbag or briefcase should be to scale - don't go too large. Add jewellery to match your top.

7. Take care with visible body piercing as this may not be appropriate.

Clothes 'talk' so therefore your image is a vitally important component and could improve your chances of getting ahead in your career.

DOES MY BUM LOOK BIG IN THIS?

Answer these questions for a mini image audit:

1. How would other people describe you?

2. When was the last time you did an audit of your wardrobe?

3. Does your image appropriately reflect the level of career/business success you'd like to achieve?

If you'd like to create a first impression worth a second look then Log onto *www.theimagepractice.co.uk* to find out more about improving your image.

Case Study: My Brother Won't Cut His Hair

One of my clients was referred to me by his sister who was at her wits' end with her brother. He had been offered a job in the family firm on one condition – that he had his hair cut. This may sound relatively straightforward but the problem here was that his hair was below his waist! And he was refusing to get it cut. No amount of pleading or nagging by his family would persuade him to get his hair cut. Although he was in a career that he no longer had any enthusiasm for and he knew that he needed to make some changes because he was stuck in a rut.

The very first thing he said to me when I spoke to him on the phone was, "You're not going to make me cut my hair are you?"

My work with him centred on his feelings about his long hair and without going into too much detail we established that because he'd had long hair since he was a child it was almost part of his identity. An identity that he was refusing to let go of. My job was to handle the stand-off that had developed between him and the rest of the family.

Eventually we did work out what was stopping him from getting his hair cut and what long hair represented for him. I did a lot of work with him using EFT (Emotional Freedom Technique). Using this technique enabled him to understand for himself what the hair really represented – the comfort and security of his childhood. I used EFT because these feelings created a block which normally would take months, even years to get through using conventional methods.

Miraculously after only our second coaching session he announced, "You know what, I'm going to get my hair cut, right now!" and immediately took himself off to the barbers and phoned me back a couple of hours later with a full report! To this day his hair remains resolutely short. He was then offered the job in the family firm and was made a member of the management team six months later. He's made a ton of new friends and is really happy. Before then even though he was stubbornly holding onto his long hair he actually didn't like himself every much and had very few friends.

"Just thought I'd let you know my aunt has told me that I am now a fully fledged member of the management team. Also I have just come back from a fantastic holiday in Malaysia, something I would only dream about before. So life is going great and I owe it all to you! I am a completely changed person. I have a whole new circle of friends, even people who knew me before and wouldn't touch me with a barge pole are now friends of mine because I am no longer that weird guy with long hair! As I said, I am a completely new person and I like the new me. Thanks again for what you did for me. I love who I am now."

TAKE A TIP FROM FLAMENCO
(EVEN IF YOU'RE A FELLA!)

Have you ever stood up to give a presentation in front of a room of 80 people with a few VIPs in the front row, all of whom are looking at you as if you've just landed from Mars? And was there at least one person sitting there with their arms folded waiting for you to fall flat on your face? How would you 'wow' them when you know that a percentage of the audience are silently thinking, "So, tell me something new; tell me something I don't already know."

Well let's go to Spain to find out.

In Flamenco the teachers are obsessed with posture Why? Because Flamenco is all about 'presence'. You feel a Flamenco dancer's presence as they walk into the room. I'd go as far as to say that you sense it before they even arrive!

'Presence' is particularly important when delivering a presentation and is one of the most dynamic tools you have to get your audience to sit up and take notice. Becoming a more dynamic version of yourself is the first step to getting an audience on your side.

So, are you ready to learn from a master?

The first step is within your breathing. Take a nice deep breath.

Stand up, feet slightly apart. Imagine that your head is being pulled up by an invisible piece of string. Now breathe through your nose, look straight ahead and stick your chest out! Hold your arms calmly by your sides. Relax and think: "I'm the best there is and I conquer all before me. I am indestructible."

Flamenco dancers exude this quality all the time - it's in their bones. Flamenco is all about intensity, power and passion. Flamenco is not for wimps. Marshal arts experts use a similar technique which helps them to ground themselves and focus their mind as they prepare to meet their opponent.

I had first-hand experience of this when I went to Jerez in Spain to be taught Flamenco by one of the best dancers in the country. He didn't speak a word of English but the whole class was mesmerised by his presence. He was absolute dynamite.

His explosive persona conveyed the passion he felt for his craft. He was very self-assured and extremely decisive.

Dance does not involve any words. The stories conveyed through flamenco are all about love, death, passion, lust, jealousy and anger. It's all done through gestures and a look which conveys how a dancer feels inside. Do not ever underestimate the ability you have to persuade others purely by your thoughts and your intention, given life through your body language.

Our teacher was able to convey this to us through his body language and eye contact alone. Astonishing! He would prowl around the dance studio like a panther. OK it was mildly dramatic and I'm not saying that this would necessarily apply if you work in accounts, but I think you get the general idea.

Non-verbal communication speaks to us at an entirely different and more profound level.

You only have one chance to create a great first impression. So the next time you're facing 'the management' you can set the scene by preparing yourself first so you are less likely to be intimidated by the experience. The more confidence and certainty you convey, the more confidence your audience will have in you. So even if you are nervous 'act as if' you are confident (or the King of the world!) it will give you a head start.

Most people who attend a presentation either want to be entertained, to learn something new or will arrive with a certain amount of scepticism. So prepare, rehearse and believe in yourself. If you stand ready for action at least you will look like you mean business.

HOW TO DEAL WITH THE WICKED WITCH OF THE WEST AND OTHER DIFFICULT PEOPLE

"Helping the little lady along are you, my fine gentlemen? Well stay away from her, or I'll stuff a mattress with you!"
The Wicked Witch of the West

Many people have been bullied at school, by an employer or fell out big-time with a work colleague. It amazes me how somebody's body language changes when they let go of these memories and feel more confident.

Some people feel ashamed, hate themselves and find it very hard to let go of the negative feelings attached to bullying for example.

I myself was bullied out of a job and the worst part of it was that I felt absolutely powerless to do anything about

146

it, because the bullying was very insidious and underhand. But looking back and knowing what I do now, it is evident that the bully must have had a very low opinion of himself. He was only able to reinforce his feelings of importance by diverting all his attention to attacking someone else.

The following exercises can be used to neutralise the feelings you have about someone who once had or continues to have a less than beneficial impact on you.

1. Going Back in Time

Go to a quiet spot.

Meditate for a couple of minutes by sitting quietly and focus softly on a spot on the wall or on the floor.

Focus on your physical body, eyes closed with a calm expression on your face.

Focus on your breathing. Pay attention and listen as you breathe in and out for a couple of minutes

Take a deep breath and focus on your heart rate, be aware of it slowing down

If your mind wanders, allow the thought through, then let it pass out of the back of your head and say, "oh, how interesting", just let it go.

Refocus your attention on your chosen object.

Now relax and imagine that a very long piece of ribbon has been attached to your big toe and the other end is tied to a stake in the ground. Now, close your eyes and feel yourself floating up through the ceiling, up through the roof, up into the sky and way up into the atmosphere and away, far away into space. See the earth below you as you float up high into the sky and far out into space. Notice how beautiful and serene it is. Know that you are safe and that you are taking this journey for your benefit.

Imagine that you are travelling back in time. Back to the time when you were bullied.

I want you to arrive 5 minutes before a particular incident that you vividly remember. Recall how things were before the problem occurred. Now I want you to re-write history and change the outcome. Change the outcome to something that is very favourable to you. Change it to something that has a happy memory attached to it, or something that makes you feel very strong and resourceful. Run this as a short film. Perhaps you punched the bully on the nose or were able to walk away without being affected. Perhaps you see the bully falling over or walking into a door. Maybe they changed their minds when they realised that they weren't going to get anywhere with you. Make this change now. Replace the memory. Do it now.

Now, hold that feeling of triumph or satisfaction or confidence. Hold it really clearly in your mind and as you hold that feeling, feel yourself being pulled back up into the air back by the ribbon and back out into space and floating serenely and slowly, back to today. All the way back to now.

You are arriving slowly back in the room, landing softly on the floor. Now, open your eyes and as you open your eyes look around you and look at what you see and hear right now. Take a deep breath.

Now think back to that time again. Does it have the same resonance? Most people feel differently when they look at it once again.

2. Walk in Their shoes

I used the following exercise for someone who worked with a very difficult character for a few years. However, her challenge was that even though he'd left and she no longer worked for him, two years later she dreaded meeting him the street. If she saw him coming in the opposite direction she'd dive into a shop or cross the road. The thought of talking to him made her feel very anxious. Once I'd taken her through the following exercise she ended up feeling quite sorry for him, which neutralised the negative feelings she had. A few weeks later she did bump into him in the street. She was able to stop and talk to him with no problems at all. He no longer represented a threat.

Imagine that there's a chair in front of you with the bully's name on it. I want you to go and sit in that chair and become them. Shut your eyes and imagine that you are wearing their clothes and shoes. Visualise the colour, texture and feel of their clothes. Now while you are being them take a moment to think like they do. What are they saying to themselves? How do they feel? What occupies their mind? What is troubling them? What do they want from life? Now (still being them) ask what is it that they want from you? What isn't happening for them? Really get into character and feel what they feel. Notice what comes into your mind and record anything relevant.

Now float out of their body and stand back and look at them again. Now this time as yourself go and sit next to them.

What questions would you like to ask them, what do want to tell them? What's important for them to know that you didn't get the chance to say before? Pause for a moment.

Now float out of your body and stand back to look at you – but this time as an observer. I want you to observe yourself sitting next to the bully and notice how you are interacting with them, but from the detached standpoint. What's going on? What messages or feelings are you picking up? Pause again.

Having gone through this exercise reflect on what's changed for you about this now and what lessons you learned. If you can look at someone you have negative feelings about, but from an objective viewpoint, it helps to neutralise the strong feelings associated with that person.

3. Look at Them Differently

Marian was troubled by a competitor who had this habit of calling just to give chapter and verse about how successful she was, how the world was at her feet and how wonderfully everything was going for her in her business.

On hearing this Marian would feel like jumping off a cliff! She was constantly comparing herself to this other woman and it made her feel totally inadequate. So I suggested that the next time she spoke to her on the telephone or even thought about her that she imagined her competitor was only five inches tall, was wearing a funny wig and spoke with a tiny squeaky voice. This technique worked immediately and now it doesn't bother Marian any more. Try this with the annoying people in your life. At the very least it will make you laugh!

HERE'S A 6 WEEK TEST FOR SALES PEOPLE

Michael Gerber author of The E-Myth Revisited suggests: *"For the first three weeks wear a brown suit to work, a starched tan shirt, and brown tie (for men), and well polished brown shoes. Make certain that all the elements of your suit are clean and well pressed. For the following three weeks wear a navy blue suit, a well starched white shirt, a tie with red in it (a pin or a scarf with red in it for women), and highly polished black shoes.*

"The results will be dramatic: sales will go up during the second three-week period! Why? Because, as our clients have consistently discovered, blue suits outsell brown suits! And it doesn't matter who's in them."

Start noticing confidence in others. Who do you know who just has that X-Factor about them? It will be a combination of how they look, what they say, how they speak and, most importantly, how they feel about themselves. If there's someone you know who you really admire why not borrow some of their attributes and model their behaviour?

"You can spot true internal power, because the people who have it also have enormous charisma. The more self-reliance you develop, the more real power you will generate for yourself. And that will make you immensely attractive to other people."

Fiona Harrold, Life Coach

ACTION POINTS – PACKAGING

1. How would having a stronger presence benefit you personally and professionally?

2. Take a good look in the mirror – catch yourself as you walk past a shop window – is that the reflection of someone you really want to be? Are your posture, your shoes, your hair and your clothes all doing you justice?

3. Record yourself speaking and work on areas that need improvement.

4. Audit your wardrobe and be ruthless with what you find.

5. Who could help you develop your presence in a meaningful way?

Packaging Power Question
How will you feel and what will you do differently when lack of confidence is no longer an issue?

Louisa Lyons was contemplating her blond plaits and duffle coat in the reflection in the train carriage window. "Hmm, possibly not necessarily the right attire for an aspiring Chartered Accountant". Her sister Denise had been threatening to throw out some of her gear, so perhaps she could help her with a clothes audit. "I can relate to that," she mused, smiling.

She realised that her wardrobe was well overdue for an overhaul. She was still hanging onto her old life at university, but was also wearing clothes that she 'thought' were right for her role, and weren't that flattering. No wonder she wasn't being taken seriously. She suddenly got a surge of excitement about walking into the office next week dressed completely differently.

If she wanted to climb the career ladder and create some opportunities for herself she needed to make some changes. Louisa was already mentally chucking out her old clothes and planning a whole new wardrobe. That girl she'd caught a fleeting glimpse of in the shop window the other day looking back at her rather sadly, no longer existed. "Note to self, agree to shopping trip with Denise - the comfortable but completely unflattering Fair Isle jumper's got to go."

Dan was very proud of the fact that he had earned the nickname of 'Scarecrow' whilst at school. He never seemed to be able to look smart for more than five minutes. For most of his adult life none of his clothes had been anywhere near an iron, and his wife had refused to become a professional ironer. Some of his clients were shocked when they met him in person. They didn't exactly visibly flinch, but it did raise a few eyebrows. He'd given up years ago with his hair anyway, as he looked like he'd just plugged himself into the mains electricity. But then on the other hand, it was part of his brand – "Boris Johnson gets away with it…"

His wife had been pleading with him to use an ironing service for his shirts, so at least he could agree to that rather than doing daft things like ironing his shirts whilst he was still wearing them.

Tom's train was approaching Stratford. The new Olympic village came into view. He could clearly see the outline of the Olympic stadium as it took shape, silhouetted against the vast temporary lighting gantries. He'd finished chapter 4 and was feeling slightly uncomfortable, because he had to confess that he was a bit of a worrier. Some of his colleagues at work had nicknamed him

'Mr Hacker' because he was always ranting about how the country was going to the dogs. He was also incredibly fussy about grammar and spelling and drove his staff crazy with being such a perfectionist. Yes he did have a knack of looking on the dark side. "But they do laugh at my funny stories though." He reasoned "If you could call chopping the tip of your finger off with an axe, funny." He never realised how much people were influenced by his blood curdling stories.

He would make more of an effort to be more upbeat and cheerful, and as he smiled he looked to his left. An attractive uniformed ticket inspector asked to see his train ticket. He scanned her with his black eyes and was amazed at how assertive and articulate she was for such a young woman. Tom was pleased that there hadn't been any lowering of standards as far as the conduct of the rail staff were concerned. He nearly asked her out for a pizza, but then realised she might not automatically warm to a man who admitted to liking trees and who kept an axe in the shed...

"Why – it's a man, a man made of tin"
Dorothy, The Wizard of Oz

Principle 5 - Beliefs

"Beliefs are how we create reality. I'm not sure how to explain this to you in a way that makes sense. You've probably noticed that people seem to have recurring problems. Did you ever wonder why it was the same problem for each person? The person with money problems always has money problems. The person with relationship problems always has relationship problems. It's as though each person specialises in a disorder. Beliefs, unconscious or not, are creating those events. Until the beliefs that create the events are released, the events will continue to reoccur."
Joe Vitale, Spiritual Marketing

DO YOUR BELIEFS REALLY SUPPORT YOU?

So, you've finally got the promotion, and your flying high, and you've splashed out on a new phone and propelling pencil. But a new role could herald the start of yet another journey, because according to a recent article in Brainstorm Magazine, when you're on the lookout for CEO-level material you can't be too careful. Up to 40 percent of newly appointed executives leave or fail within the first six to 18 months. In fact, sometimes a newly appointed manager may suddenly lose all their confidence and start to really doubt their ability. Then their career progress might resemble a game of snakes and ladders. They may possess the technical know-how and the qualifications, but if they don't truly believe in or have some strategies to handle themselves in challenging times they may end up sabotaging their success.

YOUR BELIEFS – WHY ARE THEY THERE?

Beliefs are like the legs of a table, the roots of a tree and the foundations for a house. Therefore without strong foundations, nothing has support. Hence beliefs underpin our decisions and choices. Let's look back at history to illustrate this point.

In the middle ages the Christian church 'believed' that witchcraft was the work of the Devil and therefore anyone found practicing it was tried and usually executed. One famous victim of this was Joan of Arc who was burned at the stake because the authorities believed she was practicing heresy and witchcraft. This belief was so strong that virtually everyone who was accused of witchcraft (or even owned a black cat) was tortured and beaten until they confessed to being a witch.

So a belief can be an extremely powerful weapon but not necessarily for everyone's benefit.

In the sporting arena 'belief' plays a vital role. Prior to 1954 it was believed that the 4-minute mile was, according to physiologists of the time, dangerous to the health of any athlete who attempted to reach it.

That was until Roger Bannister ran a mile in 3 minutes, 59.4 seconds By the end of 1957 16 other athletes had equalled this achievement, a clear signal that breaking this barrier was just as much a psychological feat as a physical one.

A lot of the beliefs that we hold in our mind about ourselves are handed down to us from our parents. This includes our values and strategies for handling stress and communicating with others. Even the some of our words and phrases are handed on to us from them.

But children are like mini tape recorders and automatically absorb information non-stop whether it's useful to them or not.

This tape recorder carries on recording throughout our childhood, programming our subconscious mind to automatically respond to certain situations in specific ways. This tape recorder doesn't have a reject button either. It just keeps on recording, because children absorb information like a sponge – and cannot necessarily differentiate between the worthwhile and the useless. This information includes beliefs that might not support us and maybe even completely wrong for us. The person who gave them to us may have had good intentions but could possibly be passing on beliefs that were given to them by their parents. But what worked for them might not apply to you.

Problems could arise when this programming doesn't support you at critical moments. For instance if you have limiting beliefs about how much you are worth, the strategies you employ when asking for a pay rise may fall short; thereby sabotaging your success over and over.

Which is why there are scores of people with average ability, who have achieved phenomenal success. Whilst other hugely talented people (who on paper should have succeeded), have yet to reach their potential, even after years of striving. The only difference between them is belief. A person with average ability, can literally 'talk themselves up', and gain entry into the winners circle. They decided they were a winner, way before they were on the ascendancy. And even when faced with failure, they just kept right on going, because the one thing that made the difference was a colossal belief in themselves – even despite having the odds stacked against them.

It's easy to make excuses or blame circumstances when faced with failure rather than take action or take responsibility. You might prefer to wait for someone else to do that for you instead. You could wait a lifetime...

Self-sabotage is the override switch that kicks in the minute a situation arises which requires you to dig deep, call on the best part of yourself, move out of your comfort zone and stretch. This can be very painful for some people who have gone to the most extraordinary lengths to avoid taking on a new challenge – only for change to catch up with them later on anyway.

Robert Dilts, author of 'Sleight of Mouth' says, *"Neurologically, beliefs are associated with the limbic system and hypothalamus in the midbrain. The limbic system has been linked to both emotion and long term memory. While the limbic system is a more 'primitive' structure than the cortex of the brain in many ways, it serves to integrate information from the cortex and to regulate the autonomic nervous system (which controls basic body functions such as heart rate, body temperature, pupil dilation, etc). Because they are produced by deeper structures of the brain, beliefs produce changes in the fundamental physiological functions in the body and are responsible for many of our unconscious responses. In fact, one of the ways that we know that we really believe something is because it triggers physiological reactions; it makes our 'heart pound', our 'blood boil' or our 'skin tingle' (all effects that we cannot typically produce consciously). This is how a polygraph device is able to detect whether or not a person is 'lying'. People show a different physical reaction when they believe what they are saying than when they are 'just saying' it as a behaviour (like an actor might recite a line), or when they are being untruthful or incongruent."*

So, if you've been promoted this may introduce a whole new set of challenges, one of which may require you to lead and step into the limelight. For instance how do you handle yourself in your first meeting? What do you actually say? How do you gain everyone's respect and attention? For some people chairing their first meeting could be as much fun as their first driving test!

A new challenge can be daunting, but a well thought out plan broken down into components will take into account all the elements that are required to help you succeed. Such as:

- First make sure you look good, which will make you feel good. Invest in a good wardrobe of clothes.
- Do your homework and make sure you understand the terrain, are you swimming in friendly waters for instance?
- Discover who the important characters are and who you need to watch out for? Who are the big fish?
- Make some connections. Who will your supporters be? Who can you trust?
- What skills do you think you will need to help you grow into the role?

- What are other people's expectations of you and are they realistic and achievable?

- Don't dwell too much on the, "oh god, I'm having to start all over again when I thought I knew it all in my previous career". If that's true then look into getting some mentoring.

Are you struggling to transition from one role into another because you feel you will 'lose face' because you've lost your status and don't want to appear that you don't know everything? Feel the fear and do it anyway! If anything is worth doing its worth doing poorly to start with by making improvements and adjustments as you go along. Our lives are peppered with new beginnings with it opportunities for us to learn new things and sharpen up our skills. These in turn build your confidence.

ROCK ALL THE TIME. ROCK OFTEN. ROCK LOUD!

I worked with a client employed in the Police Force. He had broken up with his girlfriend, frequently felt really depressed, and found it difficult to shrug off feelings of despondency. His feelings about himself were all negative.

During our coaching work I established that he didn't really rate himself very highly in any area. Not only that, he actually doubted whether he would ever be a confident person. This massively limited his aspirations so was in effect settling for second best. He truly believed that confidence wasn't on the menu for him. It was as if confident people were a whole different breed or belonged to an exclusive club that he wasn't worthy to be a member of.

I needed to get him to see for himself that a lot of what he was experiencing was purely down to his programming and that his habitual thoughts were playing a big part in this. So I set him some homework. For two weeks he was to look out for role models - people who he felt were really confident. Not only that, he was to ask himself what made them appear confident.

When we met at our next coaching session we had a very interesting conversation. He had noticed that, in fact, the vast majority of the 'confident' people he saw on television were perhaps confident in one area but not in all areas. Some of these people he noticed weren't actually very confident at all. This made him realise that they were just human beings doing the best they could and that they too were fallible.

Paradoxically this homework helped him to become more confident because he could empathise with others and see that they were just human - like him - with the same challenges and anxieties. He was therefore able to talk to people on the same level and with more confidence. This confidence continues to grow every day and he is beginning to create opportunities for himself which before then just weren't there. It was if the scales had balanced themselves, and as if a weight had been lifted from his shoulders.

"No pessimist every discovered the secrets of the stars, or sailed to an uncharted land, or opened a new heaven to the human spirit."
Helen Keller, American author, activist, and lecturer and the first deaf blind person to graduate from college

THE ULTIMATE ANSWER FOR
HOPELESS PROCRASTINATORS

Martyn ran his own business, but was plagued by inertia. He was finding it incredibly tiresome sorting out his paperwork and generally getting himself organised. He also found himself slipping into negative thinking and couldn't shake this off once this took hold. He procrastinated over nearly everything and was very indecisive. Over the course of a few coaching sessions it transpired that he hated paperwork (not uncommon – who doesn't?), but he didn't want to delegate this to anyone. He was also holding himself back as far as aiming a lot higher and being more ambitious with his business. He'd almost given up on some of his aspirations, and was therefore spending more time on tasks that he found unappealing than aiming for or planning for anything really exciting and challenging. Over the course of a few weeks, he slowly took control of his time management and systems, which galvanised him into action. Thereafter, he began to see new opportunities and possibilities that he'd previously written off. He'd opened the door to let some light in, which had a knock-on effect with his motivation and meant that he didn't procrastinate so much over the 'small stuff'. His belief in himself then sky-rocketed and his whole outlook changed. He knew that out there, were bigger fish for him to catch and fry!

"Frightened? Child, you're talking to a man who's laughed in the face of death, sneered at doom, and chuckled at catastrophe… I was petrified."
The Wizard of Oz

A belief about what you're capable of can become a blind spot which we don't even know we've got. If you remember I talked earlier about blind spots and DISC behaviour assessments? You could be faithfully holding onto a belief that is so solid it could get in the way of many things and sabotage your job, your health and your relationships, because it forms part of your identity; it's a coat we wear. Sometimes there is a price to pay for having a particular belief and occasionally we will go to any lengths in order to preserve it because a belief can become comfortable and familiar. It is worth examining what our intention is with holding onto a belief. Is there a secondary gain? Is there some pain associated with letting that go? But is the pain of letting it go as painful as holding onto it?

What do you really want? In what areas of your life or work are you settling for second best?

"Bad girls realise this isn't a dress rehearsal. Real life is what you make of it. You can be bad. You can be good. You just sure as hell better be authentic."

Sarah Ban Breathnach, Author 'Simple Abundance'

I'LL NAME THAT FEELING IN ONE

Have you slid down the slippery slope and are out of touch with your real feelings?

Sometimes when my clients start telling me about themselves, they say things like: "I'm not very confident" or "I'm really bored" or "I'm selfish". They identify themselves very strongly with these global statements. What I encourage them to do is to notice what they are feeling and to get really close to the truth of these statements. Occasionally it isn't lack of confidence or boredom or selfishness that is the problem. It's actually a word that they have chosen which may actually be the wrong word! Yes, really!

When questioning them more deeply, I ask them something like: "if you could choose another word for selfish, what would that be?" And quite often if I encourage them to use a word which is just a little bit more motivational, they open up and I discover that actually there's much more to the story. For example one of my clients once said to me "I'm really selfish".

I asked him to clarify what 'selfish' actually meant to him. "I love fishing, but my girlfriend doesn't want me to go because she says it's selfish." So I asked, "Is going fishing selfish?" Of course when I said it like that – he would have to examine this statement more closely.

I questioned the validity of the statement until we worked out whether he had actually chosen the right words or if the words came straight from someone else in his life, or he'd heard it so often he even started to believe it himself. My client's girlfriend had a very good reason why she really didn't want him to go fishing, but rather than articulate what she really wanted it was easier to use a blanket statement such as "You're selfish". The words "you're selfish" were the lid on a box of something else entirely, and nothing whatsoever to do with going fishing. This then led onto an issue which existed between them, which essentially needed some attention which ultimately led to a huge breakthrough in their relationship.

Sometimes we make sweeping statements concerning our level of skill or our career. For example, "I don't like writing proposals", which when looked at a little closer translates to, "I'm not very disciplined when writing long reports, I need some help to get started".

Or, "My job doesn't inspire me", which really means "I'm spending too much time at my desk when I'd rather be meeting people who energise and motivate me because that's when I'm at my best."

Venturing into these realms is similar to being a detective. When I challenge these assumptions and probe for the truth, I use a careful questioning technique which drills down to the root of the problem. It is hugely liberating. Once the door to the truth is opened I then introduce more productive and empowering words. This sparks possibilities into their lives that weren't there before.

So, stay close to what you are feeling and then ask yourself: "Is this what I am really feeling?" Drill down deeper, be frank with yourself and choose another word (or phrase) instead which reflects your true intent.

WHEN THE GOING GETS TOUGH, THE TOUGH STAY HOPEFUL...

A crucial element that keeps people motivated and therefore moving in the right direction is hope. Because when everything else is gone, sometimes hope can salvage even the most dire situation.

We've already established that pure academic ability isn't all you need to reach the top and according to Daniel Goleman hope is another ingredient that predicts success. When you're feeling hopeful about something, and therefore happier, and more relaxed it's easier to attract opportunities towards you, because you're not attached to, or fretting about , the outcome.

Goleman says studies have shown that students with high hope set themselves higher goals and know how to work hard to attain them. Hope offers an advantage in all aspects of life, including how resilient and resourceful you are.

According to University of Kansas psychologist C. R. Snyder, hope is: *"believing you have both the will and the way to accomplish your goals, whatever they may be"*. It means not giving in to anxiety, not being a defeatist and not becoming depressed in the face of difficulty – all indicators of strong emotional literacy.

Let's take redundancy for example. The thought of trying something completely different from the sort of career you've had for the last 20-odd years will be slightly daunting. The antidote to this is to take action, create possibilities and re-engineer your own future; because when you're taking action and therefore moving forward you are creating hope for yourself. And those people who talk about making their own luck 'create' opportunities for themselves at the same time.

"Whatever the limiting belief you have, it is never too late to change them, and to create a high level of self-belief. And when you believe in yourself totally and with conviction – then you will be able to do and achieve anything you wish."
Fiona Harrold, Life Coach

HOW WINSTON CHURCHILL SAVED MY LIFE

But what else do you need to create your own luck? Is there another 'intangible' that plays a crucial role in this process? How do you know what path to choose, or having chosen it, whether it's the right one? You could say that the brother or sister of hope is intuition. This skill is vastly under-rated and research has proven that people who follow their instincts are far luckier than people who don't.

According to Dr Richard Wiseman in his book 'The Luck Factor': *"Your instincts play a huge part in whether or not you will be successful or not. A very large percentage of lucky people used their intuition when making decisions in two of the four areas mentioned on the questionnaire. Almost 90% of lucky people said that they trusted their intuition when it came to their personal relationships, and almost 80% said that it played a vital role in their career choices. Perhaps more important, a greater percentage of lucky than unlucky people reported trusting their intuition in all four areas."*

Now the jury is still out as to whether intuition (and coincidences) actually exists and the argument rages on between whether it's a load of nonsense or in fact a very important characteristic of successful people. But what evidence do we have to support the argument? Your intuition is basically a huge database of experiences that you are able to references with phenomenal speed to help you in decision making. Sure you could sit down with a pen and paper and write loads of lists and then make a detailed analysis, but 9 times out of 10 all you'd need to do would be to pay attention to that voice that's saying 'I don't feel comfortable with taking this particular course of action, I don't know why, but it's strong enough for me to be concerned'. Here you are able to access that part of your brain which stores all your life experiences, which does the job of the list writing exercise at lightening speed. When faced with having to make a split second choice, (which we all have to make from time to time), it's nearly always gut instinct which wins out. In some circumstances you wouldn't have time to write any lists then anyway – like that time when you stuck your arm out to catch that glass just before it fell out of the cupboard onto the floor, or calculating whether or not you had enough time to race to platform at the railway station before your train left.

In Wiseman's book he proves that in fact lucky people do exist and they all exhibit very similar characteristics, one of which is intuition. My own experience of intuition varies from the mundane to the bizarre, as the following true story will illustrate.

It was a rainy Saturday afternoon and I was contemplating an exciting afternoon at the launderette (not!). A fairly harmless exercise, I imagined; put washing in machine, insert coins, watch machine for an hour or so, dry clothes and leave.

I bundled my washing into the machine by the window and turned to a book about ghosts and my favourite chapter about Winston Churchill. During the Second World War he often dictated speeches, memos and letters to his secretary while lying propped up in bed in the morning or late in the evening, in Downing Street's second-floor flat.

By October 1940 the Blitz began. On 14 October a huge bomb fell on Treasury Green near Downing Street, damaging the Number 10 kitchen and state rooms and killing three civil servants doing Home Guard duty.

Churchill was dining in the Garden Rooms when the air raid began. He recalled:

"We were dining in the garden-room of Number 10 when the usual night raid began. The steel shutters had been closed. Several loud explosions occurred around us at no great distance and presently a bomb fell, perhaps a hundred yards away, on the Horse Guards Parade, making a great deal of noise.

"Suddenly I had a provincial impulse. The kitchen in Number 10 Downing Street is lofty and spacious and looks out through a large plate-glass window about 25 feet high. The butler and parlour maid continued to serve the dinner with complete detachment, but I became acutely aware of this big window. I got up abruptly, went into the kitchen, told the butler to put the dinner on the hot plate in the dining-room and ordered the cook and the other servants into the shelter, such as it was.

"I had been seated again at the table only about three minutes when a really loud crash, close at hand and a violent shock showed that the house had been struck. My detective came into the room and said much damage had been done. The kitchen, the pantry and the offices on the Treasury were shattered."

Winston Churchill made many decisions guided by his intuition. He'd undoubtedly saved a few lives that afternoon by listening to a quiet voice.

I'd just reached the end of that particular chapter of the book, when a loud BOOM split the air. I looked to my right and not six feet away, a dark green Austin Montego had crashed through the plate glass window of the shop! The female driver sat staring through the windscreen like a participant at a hypnotist's show.

Then I looked down at my feet and saw a large chunk of green plate glass lying on the floor. I did the sums, plate glass, one inch thick, the size of a breadboard, weighing approximately 5 kilos, with a terminal velocity of 50 mph at a trajectory of…

A siren blasted out and the police arrived. A policeman marched efficiently into the launderette (through a door that still had glass in it) and announced into his two-way radio, "Nah, Sarge! Nothing much here. Car's gone through a window. Nobody died."

My washing eventually reached the tumble dryer. Although I had to wait for the firemen to jack the car out of the shop before I could retrieve my washing from the machine.

From one point of view however it was a blessing that the wash cycle took a very long time. It would have been a different story had the driver of the Austin put the keys into the ignition of her car at the precise moment I chose to unload my washing from the machine by the window.

Would you say it was a coincidence? There was certainly a message in that book for me, for which I have absolutely no explanation. The only thing I would say is that for some reason I was compelled to sit and read that particular chapter, rather than spend the afternoon on my feet walking around and being a target for anything coming through the window.

You may find yourself going somewhere or may feel 'prompted' to call someone for no apparent reason, only because you 'feel you should'. As I said before, the subconscious mind is more powerful than we realise, so pay attention. Not only could intuition save your life, it could also manifest opportunities and attract into your life coincidences and people who may be very influential to you and your future.

Pause and let's rewind for a moment...

Choose to give back unsupportive beliefs and replace them with something more empowering. After all, who said you had to keep them?

Think of a scenario where you are regularly using the words "I can't". Ask yourself this question – how do you know that to be true? Where's your evidence? And what would happen if you said, "I can" instead?

It is human nature to stay with what is comfortable and familiar and to be deeply suspicious of anything that threatens the status quo. It's the brave person who is willing to challenge their own assumptions and do something different. As Anthony Robbins puts it: *"Take appropriate risks: Sometimes reaching your goals will require that you take risks you're really uncomfortable with. Change is an uncomfortable state; we all want certainty and security in our lives. But if you don't take the risks, you may not reach your goal. Make a decision to break out of your comfort zone. Get support when needed."*

PERSONAL WORKSHOP ACTIVITY
- BELIEFS ASSESSMENT SHEET

Write down a one-sentence description of your goal to be achieved. For example, get out of the rat race, gain a promotion, retire happily, learn a new skill, ask for a pay rise.

Goal/Outcome

In the spaces provided below, rate your degree of belief in the outcome in relation to each of the statements on a scale of 1 to 5, with 1 being the lowest and 5 being the highest degree of belief.

The goal is desirable and worth it

 ❑1 ❑2 ❑3 ❑4 ❑5

It is possible to achieve the goal

 ❑1 ❑2 ❑3 ❑4 ❑5

What has to be done in order to achieve the goal is appropriate and ecological?

 ❑1 ❑2 ❑3 ❑4 ❑5

I have the capabilities necessary to achieve the goal

 ❑1 ❑2 ❑3 ❑4 ❑5

I have the responsibility and deserve to achieve the goal

 ❑1 ❑2 ❑3 ❑4 ❑5

Building Confidence and Strengthening Belief

Once you have assessed your degree of confidence and congruence with respect to these key areas of belief you can strengthen your belief in areas of doubt by considering the following questions:

1. What else would you need to know, add to your goal or believe in order to be more congruent or confident?

2. Who would be your mentor for that belief?

3. What message or advice would that mentor have for you?

LESSONS FROM THE OLYMPICS

How did athletics turn a slightly deaf, backward, painfully shy girl into a school celebrity? I was lucky to have a natural talent for sprinting and I am absolutely convinced that it supercharged my academic performance. I still advocate exercise for children for getting their little brains in gear. I find it astonishing that we wonder why there has been an explosion in behavioural problems in children at the moment. Children don't have the freedom to play outside as they used to, instead they spend too much time in front of a computer. Activities that are crucial to their development such as play, art, sport and music have only recently been given higher status.

Plus what does the testing regime in our schools actually achieve? You can't test a child's imagination, their personality, their aspirations, their love of life or how many times a day they laugh can you? We test nuclear reactors and cars – how does that apply to children??

And then if that isn't enough, the rest of the time parents are hovering over their offspring protectively just in case something dreadful happens to them, programming their children to be more or less fearful of everything. Oh dear me.

I was an extremely slow learner and did incredibly badly at school academically. However, the turning point came when I discovered I was actually a gifted athlete. I'd never competed in any sports at school as I was too shy. Every year I would hide behind some trees watching the events, or just go home. Eventually one of the teachers caught up with me in the playground one day and persuaded me to compete at the last ever sports day before I left to join secondary school in September. He just said, "Wendy it's your last chance…"

I do believe that at important turning points in our lives significant people step forward with the power to change our destiny. It is up to us to recognise these people and act accordingly.

On the day of the race I was so clueless about the whole running thing I even had to ask the old codger in the white blazer what to do as he stood there with the starting gun. "Just stand there and when I fire this gun, run like hell!" he boomed.

Well, I destroyed the opposition in my very first race. It was run on grass and I was wearing plimsolls. I crashed through the tape a full three seconds before everyone else. My school days would never be quite the same again.

As I write the Beijing Olympics has just drawn to a close. And, in keeping with the Games, it has brought with it the usual stories of triumph and disaster. For example the British and American relay teams were disqualified, the Chinese hurdler withdrew from the final of the 100m hurdles through injury and Chris Hoy was the first British cyclist for 100 years to win three gold medals at an Olympics.

For nearly every competitor there is a story behind their success. Apparently Michael Phelps took up swimming after being diagnosed with ADHD when he was a child never realising that one day he would become an Olympic gold medallist several times over. Many athletes have overcome huge disappointment, setbacks and delays or made significant personal sacrifices on the way to winning a medal. Some will have returned home with nothing to show for all their dedication.

My athletic career almost came to a grinding halt before it had even got started! At 14 years of age I was taken to the local Athletics stadium for a trial to represent Essex in the 100 metres at the Southern Counties Championships. To cut a long story short, heavy rain and a cinder track (black soot to you and me) don't mix so, unbelievably, I slipped and fell flat on my face at the start of the race and I finished last.

To say that I was speechless with disappointment was the understatement of the year. Anyway I went away, regrouped and after talking it over with my coach I secured a place in the sprint relay team instead and eventually made it to the championships. He also suggested that I try the long jump as an individual event, which I did. I surpassed my personal best. I eventually moved on from athletics but I still have very good feelings attached to the sport which helped to build my self confidence which for a kid with my background was very gratifying.

If you'd like something in your armoury to help you focus on achievement and succeed, I've 'borrowed' 10 Top Tips from the world of Athletics that you might find useful.

Faster, Higher, Stronger

1. Be prepared and get the tools you need to get the job done.
2. Be flexible, if things don't work out quite the way you planned, regroup and think it over.
3. Talk it over with a trusted adviser and get their slant on things, and listen.
4. Be tenacious - eventually you will be rewarded.
5. Focus on your objective - ignore the competition - what matters is you, how you feel about yourself and your own performance.
6. Reach for much more than you think you're capable of. Aim as high as you possibly can.
7. Turn up, show up and do your best no matter what the conditions or the circumstances.
8. Give it just one more degree of effort. Anyone can take the easy route and give up - and you're not just anyone, are you?
9. Think about what didn't work and try a new approach.
10. Get over it and move on - failure happens to even the most talented people.

SUCCESS ISN'T ALL IN THE MIND

Some people may struggle with the notion of positive thinking because their beliefs about their lack of ability are too deeply embedded. Doubt will pepper their thoughts and their conversation. And the strangest part of this is that when I coach people who feel like this I can almost see the face of the person who planted the seeds of doubt in their mind, as they talk to me. Doubt about an outcome can strike at any age and may suddenly take hold with such force that a formerly extremely confident person may suddenly start to behave differently. Old memories may return.

Fortunately I came across EFT (Emotional Freedom Technique) on an NLP training course which helped me overcome severe claustrophobia. I then went on to do the training myself and came to the incredible realisation that in fact, removing obstacles is less to do with willpower or forcing yourself to 'overcome' but more akin to tuning into what your body is telling you.

The thinking behind EFT is that the cause of all negative emotion is a disruption in the energy meridians of the body. Roger Callaghan - a respected psychotherapist in the USA - discovered that there was a link between the meridians in the body (as used in acupuncture) and the way people feel. His original idea was formulated into TFT (Thought Field Therapy) and later developed into EFT by Gary Craig. EFT uses a tapping technique which is a marriage of Eastern acupuncture (without the needles, of course) and Western kinesiology.

EFT is different from Counselling. Counselling involves talking about a memory or something that concerns you to identify how you feel and why you feel the way you do. Whereas EFT uses a different approach. Instead when you combine talking with tapping on the meridians this has a beneficial effect on your body, not just your mind and adjusts the flow of energy.

For EFT to work properly however, you have to 'tune into' the memory. Only by tuning in can I get an accurate idea of how strongly someone is affected by a particular event. Firstly, I take a SUDS reading (Subjective Unit of Distress) from between 0 – 10 (10 being high anxiety/concern).

Between each 'round' of tapping this number usually reduces, with the aim to reach either 1 or zero – this is often easily achievable.

TFT and EFT have been developed steadily over the past 30-odd years and are at the forefront of new therapies. EFT combines fantastically well with NLP and uses a similar approach. As Richard Bandler puts it, NLP is more about observing behaviour and less analysis which is where being very intuitive works so well.

This is what differentiates counselling, psychiatry and psychotherapy from newer therapies like EFT which take an entirely different and much more intuitive route. EFT professionals don't make any assumptions or resort to lengthy analysis as to why someone thinks or behaves in a certain way. In many cases neither I nor my clients have any idea what the core issue is at the outset. EFT uncovers each layer which may obscure the core issue. It's totally fascinating.

Sometimes the negative emotions associated with these old memories can be released completely within a very short period of time using EFT, even in just an hour! It works because EFT accesses both sides of the brain (logical left hand side and emotional right hand side) and somehow helps to unscramble the mind, enabling the client to recall a memory or an experience but without the negative emotions associated with it. When under stress the emotional side of the brain paralyses the logical side, making it very difficult to see clearly or make rational, balanced decisions.

The Cause of All Negative Emotion is a Disruption in the Energy Meridians of the Body

EFT Case Study: When Fear Gets in The Way

Why getting your dream job could be the scariest thing that's ever happened to you...

Angela had been offered the job of a lifetime in London, which was absolutely tailor-made for her. But she was petrified of making the leap to commuting to London, using the underground, changing her routine and grasping the opportunity. We had only two weeks to work on this challenge, so the clock was ticking. It wasn't up to me to tell her to take the job, but we had work to do to help her to see it as an opportunity rather than a scary obstacle. I eventually discovered the root cause of her fears, which were dissolved with EFT. She then went on to accept the vacancy.

"I met Wendy at a time when I had to make some considerable – and unwelcome – changes to my life. I was frightened and stressed, and my husband suggested Wendy might be able to help. I have never found it easy to admit to having problems, and so I approached our first meeting with some trepidation. I needn't have worried. Wendy is a kind and thoughtful person who listened to me quietly and without judgement, which in itself I found calming and reassuring. A series of practical exercises helped me to understand my own feelings and fears,

and gave me the tools to take control and move forward in a positive way. Her 'tapping' technique got me through many a bad moment and I still use it regularly.

"To take one very practical example: I had a big fear of travelling by tube which, in the past, had resulted in some very unpleasant panic attacks. On a daily basis I now pack myself onto a crowded Central Line tube train with no more than a sigh of resignation - something Wendy helped me to achieve."

Log onto my website at *www.resolutioncoaching.co.uk* or www.emofree.com to find out more about EFT.

Occasionally however, we know we want to change but however hard we try we seem to slip back into old habits and patterns of behaviour. This isn't uncommon in some people. However, changes can be brought about by a number of methods; repetition over a period of time, a massive emotional input which, like a rocket, fires you on to a new level. One method which can help individuals learn to use the unlimited resources in their subconscious mind is through hypnotherapy.

Hypnotherapy is simply a way to help you get in touch with your subconscious through hypnosis which, contrary to popular belief, is just a particular type of relaxation. In hypnosis the mind is in a more creative learning state than in normal wakefulness and is open to beneficial ideas. Changes can often take place very rapidly. At other times the experience is more of a process where you have an enhanced sense of choice. Something happens that in the past has pushed your buttons, but you find yourself momentarily hesitating and instead of reacting in the same old way you choose to do something different and more beneficial instead. It's a bit like learning to play the piano. New neural pathways have to be created and well used until the new behaviour becomes automatic.

To find out more about hypnosis and hypnotherapy visit *www.lifechangesnow.co.uk*

"I am the greatest. I said that even before I knew I was. Don't tell me I can't do something. Don't tell me it's impossible. Don't tell me I'm not the greatest. I'm the double greatest."
Muhammad Ali, Professional Boxer

ACTION POINTS - BELIEFS

1. What beliefs are getting in the way of your progress and blocking your path?
2. Who could help you to modify them to help you grasp more opportunities?
3. Take a few minutes to list these and work on them one at a time.
4. Start today.

Beliefs Power Question
Which statement is true?
"I'll believe it when I see it"
or "I'll see it when I believe it"?

Tom was struck how, for the past 25 years he'd been in a role which accurately reflected his level of training and expertise. He'd successfully studied and gained many qualifications to reach this level, however, when he recalled his decision to enter into reinsurance there had been a smaller voice that had called out to him then, that he'd completely ignored. He'd ignored it because he didn't believe he could succeed in this other role, namely in horticulture and garden design. He was absorbed by plants and trees, creating things out of wood and had a fascination with design, colour and form. Here he was in another world - completely content.

The only person who'd ever doubted his ability to succeed in this area was his father. And of course having matured and reflected on his life he knew that although his father meant well, in fact he didn't really understand because he had absolutely no interest in the great outdoors. For a moment Tom felt a pang of regret and annoyance at not following his dream. He had allowed other people to dictate his path for him. Years later here he was 'solid reliable Tom' – a 45 year old oak tree. He had become so dependable in the office that he was literally part of the furniture. This was why he was sitting on this train, looking into the void and why he'd been given this book.

Louisa's train was approaching her stop. She didn't want to stop reading because she'd suddenly stumbled upon a missing piece of her life puzzle. Her whole experience of life up until this point had been one of being compliant or waiting for other people to give her the green light to do this or that. She decided that she'd had enough of being treated like a beginner by her boss 'The Wicked Witch of the West'. She was so frantic to fit in that she'd become invisible and therefore a complete walk-over. She was assigned tasks and projects that didn't showcase her ability and didn't look good on a CV! She suddenly felt really angry.

As the train trundled towards her station she resolved to demand much more at work. To boost her confidence she would go to all her friends and ask them: "Tell me, what's great, unique and special about me?"

Dan stared into the fire. He remembered his mother saying, "You're a control freak". She despaired at her son who was an absolute nightmare at school. Desperate to cover up the fact that he couldn't read properly he'd employed numerous strategies to avoid detection, which included a total disregard for authority and a reluctance to tow the line in any way.

Fortunately being a resourceful boy he'd got by through sport and being very entrepreneurial. His first venture involved buying sweets at the cash and carry and selling them in the playground. He had an aggressive attitude which carried through into his career, and he resented anyone being in control of him. But whilst he was busy doing that – he was actually controlling everyone else!

It was only recently that he'd discovered he was dyslexic – which was a big weight off his mind. Still, old habits die-hard. Fortunately he had a PA who could see right through him and when he was going into control freak mode, she smiled knowingly. But even she despaired as she watched her boss working himself into a frazzle and micro-managing everyone. Dan smiled for the first time that day. "So, I'm a recovering dyslexic, moronic loser. The only way is up."

Principle 6 - Values

"A Heart is not judged by how much you love, but by how much you are loved."
Professor Marvel, The Wizard of Oz

WELCOME TO VENETIA

Have you ever walked out of a restaurant in disgust at the poor treatment you've received, vowing never to return because the soup was cold and the service was sloppy? Have you ever fallen out with a friend you've known for years after they let you down once too often? Have you ever not taken a job because something about the company "didn't feel right"? Here we have examples of a clash of values.

It's pleasing to visit establishments (like restaurants and hotels, for instance) who take care of the little things. Like being courteous, making sure everything is spotless, staff that smile at you and ask you how you are. You feel that essentially at the heart of their organisation is someone who cares.

If you are finding it difficult to get excited about your job then perhaps it's because your values have been compromised or you and what you stand for don't belong there.

Your values and beliefs are the stake in the ground, the bedrock of who you are. It's the glue that holds everything together - including your relationships - and if you own a business, it forms part of your brand, your message, your principles and your mission. It's you personified. It's where some people get the opportunity to showcase what they care about or to devote themselves to a cause that really matters to them.

I am sure I am not the only person who has looked on in dismay at the gradual erosion of our cultural values, which have unfortunately been replaced by rampant consumerism and the 'get rich quick' society. I know I've been there myself. I've been to a shopping mall and spent £500 in an afternoon on clothes and come out in a cold sweat thinking, "how did that happen?" Marketing techniques have become so sophisticated that going to the supermarket isn't just about buying food any more. You go to the supermarket for a loaf and come out with a toaster and a two bottles of champagne because is BOGOF week!

"Women shouldn't judge the success of their business on traditional values. If one of your business objectives is to have the time to meet your child at the school gate, or spend time with your family, that's fine. You aim might not necessarily be to grow your business, but to make it more effective and therefore more profitable."
Liz Lake, Chartered Architect and Director, Liz Lake Chartered Landscape Architects and Urban Designers

Think about incidents in your life that you've felt strongly about (both positive and negative). Perhaps it's being late for appointments, telling lies, queuing, gossiping, honouring agreements, injustice, the environment, giving to charity, a decent education, dignity and fair play – what's important to you about that? Whatever it is that is important to you says a lot about you and your values. Knowing what you want - and why it's important - shapes who you are and what you stand for.

Michael Gerber calls this Your Primary aim. In his book 'The E-Myth Revisited', he tells us about his experience of staying at The Venetia Hotel on the Pacific Coast. I'd love to stay at this establishment because his experience from beginning to end sounds nothing less than first class. From the way the hotel staff greeted him on his arrival, to the appointment of his room, the food and how the staff paid attention to tailor everything to ensure he was very well taken care of. They even took the time to find out what newspaper he liked to read in the morning and his favourite brand of coffee so that these were provided for him as a matter of course. They cared enough to put effort into the experience. They supplied, in Michael's words, *"an orchestrated solution designed to produce a marketing result, an integrated component of the hotel's Management System"*.

This is a clear demonstration of an organisation which is underpinned by very clear values and is a reflection of the person who had the vision, the will, the organisation and the dedication to make it happen.

Consider this for a minute. If you have found yourself struggling with lack of motivation could it be that you haven't clearly discovered what your highest and best purpose in life is? Sadly some people never make that connection, and then wonder why they have to eat half a ton of chocolate every night in front of the Telly.

Strengthening your values, having an opinion and speaking with conviction about what you care about, carries more weight than someone who changes their mind every five minutes or spends their entire life compromising.

For me freedom of expression is particularly important and being given a platform upon which to state what I think without contradiction or ridicule. I don't want to be labelled or pigeon-holed by smaller minds who have different values. I feel it's fatal to be defined by someone who doesn't appreciate or empathise with issues that I feel passionate about. Sadly, some people will go a long way to preserve the status quo and accept mediocrity and compromise without question rather than embracing new concepts.

Stop for a minute and identify what things are really important to you in your life and then ask yourself why that is important to you? Even organisations that write mission or vision statements discover that these documents end up in a drawer somewhere because the person who devised them doesn't live by the vision himself and hasn't engaged with the people they were written for either. If it ticks a box for compliance reasons then that's fine. However, if compliance means everyone has to subscribe to the company values when neither side actually really believes them, it could prove counter-productive and a waste of time and money in the long run.

Being clear on your values is the cornerstone of integrity. It's not enough to just talk about values, anyone can do that. You have to demonstrate that you are living your life and running your business by strong guiding principles. It's having a set of values that you are prepared to stand by when it counts. It's honouring people in their absence or being consistent with your message. It's demonstrating that you have standards that you are prepared to live up to.

OZ HAS SPOKEN

And it doesn't mean being perfect or demonstrating how generous you are with grand gestures either. It's the little things that count almost as much like remembering birthdays, smiling and saying hello to a stranger, going out of your way for someone when you don't really feel like it. Random acts of kindness, doing things for other people when you know there's nothing in it for you. Taking time out of your schedule to listen to someone or help them when you'd rather be somewhere else.

In The Wizard of Oz, when Dorothy, the Lion, the Tin man and the Scarecrow reach the Emerald City they discover that the Great Oz is in fact a conman and the Great Oz doesn't actually exist. He'd devised an elaborate scam to convince everyone in the Emerald City that he was an all-powerful super being, when in reality he was a ventriloquist from Omaha.

I remember years ago I was the chairman of a committee and I decided that when we held meetings it was polite to allow each person to speak without being interrupted by several people speaking simultaneously. This caused a storm of protest and at the meeting I was completely savaged for standing up for what I believed in. Sometimes it's hard to say what you think for fear of the consequences. It is sad that yes some people will judge

190

you, hurt you or turn their back on you and let you down. But the most exciting, the most powerful people I know, have such strong values that they are like oak trees. Nothing knocks them or fazes them because they aren't afraid to have the courage of their convictions when it matters. They don't need an audience or a round of applause every time they do something laudable either.

Anyone can be mediocre, anyone can run with the pack, but hopefully you'd rather be a lion for a day than a sheep for your whole life.

BECOMING AWARE OF YOUR DEEPEST VALUES

Steve Andreas and Charles Faulkner, state in their book "The New Technology of Achievement", that there are three ways that people become aware of their deep values.

The most common examples would be when something happens that makes us feel either very angry, upset or uncomfortable. Values usually surface if they are accompanied by strong feeling, for example when someone is constantly arriving late for meetings.

One thing that really infuriates me is when people drop litter. I have been known to pick up the litter, follow the culprit up the road and give it back to them and then to say, "excuse me, I think you dropped this. It belongs in the rubbish bin which I think you'll find is over there". They are usually so shocked they can find nothing to say and usually comply without question.

When our values are challenged or not honoured we may get angry or upset. For instance, you may feel strongly about honesty and fair play, common courtesy, human rights, privacy, grammar, honour and dignity, culture and tradition, family ties, family heritage, recycling, smoking, nudity. Everyone has something that they feel strongly about which points to their particular value system.

As Andreas and Faulkner point out another way to connect with your values is through events that fulfil them. Values are sets of feelings that let you know what is important to you. This could occur at times of great happiness such as being inspired by musical performances or watching outstanding sporting achievements. Our feelings are the key indicator here. For example I knew at the age of 10 that I wanted to be a cellist after my father took me to the opera. I sat transfixed throughout the entire performance. Classical music is still extremely important to me, as are the personal triumphs and tragedies behind the composers who wrote the music.

Take Beethoven as an example. Even though he knew he was becoming irreversibly, profoundly deaf he continued to compose. This was so distressing for him that he contemplated suicide numerous times, but each time would come back from the brink with a musical creation of unmatched genius. By the time of his death, he'd touched so many people with his music that it is estimated between 10,000 to 30,000 people attended his funeral.

Another way to experience our deep values is through conscious inner exploration. It is sometimes through deep meditation that we can discover and feel our deepest values. And it is sometimes in those moments of stillness, like when sitting on the beach or even waiting for a train, that you can connect with these inner thoughts. We are usually too busy rushing around to fully connect with them.

Lastly, the next thing to do with your values and principles is to connect them to a grand vision of a distinguished life – through a mission of change, an inspiring creative project, using a personal experience to become a voice on behalf of other people or committing yourself to a cause.

PERSONAL WORKSHOP ACTIVITY - GET INSPIRED

Write a list of your top 5 favourite motivational films.

Identify the theme of these films and what really inspired you about them. What is important to you about the characters and their experiences?

From here you will be able to identify what's important to you. Highlight the key words that are revealed in this exercise – a key factor in determining what your values are.

Ask yourself, are these values part of your life right now, and if not what could you do to incorporate them into your life?

Three of my favourite films include:

The 39 Steps - Richard Hannay is a Canadian visitor to 1930's London. At the end of "Mr Memory's" show in a music hall, he meets Annabella Smith who is on the run from foreign agents. He takes her back to his apartment, but they are followed and later that night Annabella is murdered. Hannay goes on the run to break the spy ring and thus prove his innocence.

What I like about this film (apart from being hugely entertaining) is the central character's epic and unrelenting efforts to expose the truth.

Star Man - Having accepted an invitation to visit Earth (sent in the one of the Voyager space probes in the 1970s), an alien crash-lands in the United States and takes on the appearance of a woman's dead husband and enlists her help to escape from pursuing authorities. As he learns how to be more human the alien begins to take on more and more qualities of the woman's husband, drawing the woman closer.

I adore this film, because through the human experience the alien discovers what makes life endurable and meaningful - is love.

The China Syndrome - While doing a series of reports on alternative energy sources, an opportunistic reporter Kimberly Wells witnesses an accident at a nuclear power plant. Wells is determined to publicise the incident but soon finds herself entangled in a sinister conspiracy to keep the full impact of the incident a secret.

Standing up for and doing the right thing is the key message for me in this film – as the trailer said: "Sometimes the right thing to do, is the hardest thing to do."

"Answering the call to live our life's purpose is inevitable and, once we respond, there is no turning back."
Nick Williams, The Work We Were Born To Do

194

ACTION POINTS - VALUES

Ask yourself:

- Has the excitement gone from your life and career?
- What could you do instead that really fires you up?
- Who are your role models?
- What strengths can you 'borrow' from them that might make a difference to you?
- Where are you tolerating that signifies that your values are being compromised?

Values Power Question

What's important to you about success?
What will that get you?

Tom watched the scenery flash past the train as he sped home. He felt the impact of the last chapter like an electric shock. He recalled the decisions he'd made where he'd not really believed what he was doing. Now 20 years later, having put all his eggs in one basket, he'd not really moved on personally at all. He was beginning to suspect that the perception others had of him was of someone who didn't really have very high expectations of life at all. Maybe it was time for him to have a personal renaissance and grab a piece of life for himself before it was too late. The trees beckoned.

Dan was wondering why he was still the only person in the pub. "Where was everyone?" He was totally alone, apart from the barman and a strange little black dog that had taken up residence on Dan's foot. He found the warmth of the little creature strangely comforting. He reached the next chapter and oddly by then had no desire to order another large Jack Daniels. Dan's obsession with achievement at all costs had cost him his health. It was only because he woke up this morning in the most excruciating pain that forced him to go to the doctor. He'd hit a brick wall and had to admit that he didn't like this feeling of being out of control at all. But, he reasoned, the same mindset that brought him success would be the same one that would systematically go about rearranging his priorities so he didn't end up in the emergency room. He thought that perhaps he needed a diversion to slow him down a bit, like a dog for instance...

"What's the dog's name?" he barked at the Barman. "Dunno – he just walked in here when you did. I thought he was yours..."

Louisa pondered as to why, when she was on the hockey pitch she was more or less invincible. She'd suffered numerous black eyes, a fractured cheekbone and a split lip. However, when she was at work all that dynamism went out of the window. What was it about a hockey match that mattered so much to her that she was prepared to suffer physical pain as a result?

She reflected on her degree, and how hard she'd worked, and she'd put just as much effort into finding employment. But once she'd been hired she suddenly became really timid. One thing that really bugged her about her boss was that she looked on Louisa as if she was a child of 10, and unable to tie her own shoelaces. Sometimes she felt like everything was 'taken care' of for her to the point where as long as she processed the work, she didn't even have to think for herself, make any decisions or even think very hard.

Her domineering boss had actually stripped her of any need to use any initiative, wasn't channelling her skills or even giving her the opportunity to aim higher. "I've got the wrong boss. It's not me that's got the problem. It's her!" She grabbed her diary and wrote in big letters. "Change image. Get some feedback. Be nice to self. Get a new job."

Principle 7 - Vision

"I realised that for IBM to become a great company it would have to act like a great company long before it ever became one.

"From the very outset, IBM was fashioned after the template of my vision. And each and every day we attempted to model the company after that template. At the end of each day, we asked ourselves how well we did, discovered the disparity between where we were and where we had committed ourselves to be and, at the start of the following day, set out to make up for the difference.

"Every day at IBM was a day devoted to business development, not doing business.

"We didn't do business at IBM, we built one."
Tom Watson, Founder of IBM

ARE YOU STILL SEARCHING FOR THE EMERALD CITY?

So, where next for you? Now as you reach the final chapter in this book I hope you have begun to grasp the concepts outlined here. Perhaps you have already identified that the less interference you have in your life, either from internal or external influences, the greater your chances of success will be. And you may as well accept right now that if you want something to change in your life or career, you're going to have to be involved in the process somewhere.

I know because when things aren't going quite my way, sure enough I do have something to do with it. However, once I acknowledge this fact and then consciously work at dealing with this I gain control along with the energy and enthusiasm to move forward.

You may well have ambitions to make some radical changes to your career but if your life is cluttered with 'stuff' – like an unrewarding career, a reactive or negative attitude, a lifestyle that is unsustainable and unhealthy, unsupportive beliefs, behaviour and programming or you are unclear on your values - these will keep you from experiencing clarity on your goal. And if you don't really know what you want, where is your plan going to come from? Not only that, if you do have some sort of plan, without a clear vision, you could paradoxically be heading in completely the wrong direction (or no direction whatsoever). You could waste time if a course correction isn't made soon. Which is where this book comes in. I don't want you to look back with regret in 10 years time and think: "what HAVE I been doing, where did all those years go?" Whereas if you devise an orchestrated plan you might just start to see some tangible results.

So, let's assume that you have removed, or are taking steps to handle any interference and therefore working optimistically towards a future goal.

Are you one of those people who, like me, when you go out to a restaurant, goes straight to the dessert menu first? It's nice to look forward to sticky toffee pudding, or chocolate mousse, but it's normal to eat the main course first. It is important to identify your mission, but the process that I've outlined through the previous six core principles must take place before you can get to the really exciting part of your life. Put another way, you can't fly to the moon, if your space ship isn't ready, the astronauts aren't fully trained and there's no flight plan – no matter how determined you are to get there.

Some people have no idea what they could achieve because they have pointless distractions luring them away from their purpose.

Once you've got clarity and focus your choices will be congruent with your objectives. You could say that your purpose is the cherry pie in your life – but make sure you enjoy the journey to the restaurant, have savoured the right main course and there's nothing around to spoil the pie when it finally arrives.

So what else could get in your way? Sometimes we might be seduced by the trappings of success. Things like new cars, a big house, exotic holidays or designer clothes, and forget that to manifest these into our life we have to focus on something much more meaningful, because the material gains are merely a bonus. The main enjoyment should be in the work (the journey) itself, or the realisation of a long held ambition. I spent a while being confused as to my definition of success. These days we are sandblasted with marketing and advertising which could lead us to think that material gain IS success. When it is in actuality, a by-product. A big desire to attain material possessions could turn out to be yet another distraction, tempting us away from our real purpose - where true and lasting satisfaction will be found.

GET THERE FASTER, BY GOING THERE FIRST

How do you remain focussed on your objectives and bring them into reality?

Let's go back to the Olympics for a moment. Part of the training for the 10 metre diving is visualisation. They do the physical training but they are also trained in visualisation, In the last few seconds before the dive is executed, they switch off the visualisation, clear their minds and then just go for it. Competitors know that they've completed all their training but what takes over after that point is pure instinct. There appears to be a system: Training, Visualisation, Clear Your Mind, Go For it.

Scientists have been able to establish that if you rehearse something in your mind (like diving off a 10 metre diving board), you are actually firing the same signals to the relevant muscles involved as if you were actually doing it. The brain cannot differentiate between reality and imagination. My long jump coach would train me to look up and imagine myself jumping over a big oak tree which grew opposite the long jump pit where I trained.

Your goal might be to get that job, impress an audience with your presentation, hold a meeting to discuss your finances or pass an exam, you can use the visualisation exercise to rehearse the perfect outcome for any of them.

Wouldn't it be great if tomorrow you could get out of bed knowing that something you are going to do will change someone's life. Maybe you will devise a world beating innovation, or make a significant contribution to your organisation?

Surely it's more rewarding to be a part of a great new scheme and have a compelling future awaiting you?

Let other people with small minds fight and squabble amongst themselves, or spend their time flicking through catalogues or planning their next shopping trip. You are destined for bigger and juicier opportunities which will call forth a sense of achievement which far out strips anything you ever experienced in your life thus far. What I'm advocating is climbing right up to the top of the mountain, where you're breathing clearer air. Here you can see so much more and get a sense of why you're REALLY here.

PERSONAL WORKSHOP ACTIVITY
– MOTIVATING AFFIRMATIONS

The following exercise is a very powerful way of creating an affirmation to harness the combined power of the RAS system (Reticular Activating System), by using the power of repetition and defining a clear purpose.

Writing down an affirmation and reading this on a regular basis activates the RAS to bring forth what you most desire. The RAS works as the filter between your conscious and subconscious mind by filtering out sensory stimuli so that you don't get overloaded with unnecessary information. If you repeat your affirmation every day for 21 days this becomes a positive habit. However, if you've set your filter only to 'see' negative stuff, e.g. if you're in 'failure' mode, your RAS will only allow stimuli through that reinforces your 'failure' mode programming. Whereas if you have and affirm a clear picture of what you want on a regular basis this re-programmes your RAS and subtly changes your awareness to reinforce this positive programming.

This exercise has been reproduced with kind permission of Ian Parkin at *www.ianparkin.info*.

Motivating Affirmation List 1

List the ten things that you most want out of life, i.e. perfect relationship, financial security, comfortable home etc…

Motivating Affirmation List 2

List the ten things that you most want in your career or business.

Motivating Affirmation List 3

List the ten things that you believe make YOU special.

Motivating Affirmation List 4

List ten activities that you can do now in your career or business.

Now that you have completed ten items on each of your lists, please identify the one most important statement in each of the four lists.

Most important statement from List 1:

Most important statement from List 2:

Most important statement from List 3:

Most important statement from List 4:

Now compose your motivating affirmation using the selections from each of your four lists in this order.

"I am... (Choose an Activity from List 4) .... (and by) using my... (Personal Attribute from List 3) .... (and in so doing) I create... (Career Objective from List 2) .... with which I attain... (What you Most want from life in List 1) .... and everything has helped this to happen."

1. Compose and write out your affirmation.
   Here's mine:

   "I am publishing the best book on personal coaching and developing some motivational workshops and by sharing my knowledge, leading and inspiring others to help them succeed I create the opportunity to raise my profile and gain recognition for my skills, with which I attain financial reward and therefore more time to spend with my family and enjoy all my hobbies and interests. And everything has helped this to happen."

2. Print it out and paste it up in places you will see it regularly – (bathroom mirror, inside your locker, dashboard of your car, bedside note card, send it in a greeting card to yourself!)

3. Read it to yourself first thing each morning.

4. Read it to yourself last thing at night.

5. Be vigilant in reciting your motivating affirmation for at least 21 days straight - it will then become a habit.

RAS will open you up to success and automatically direct you towards the people and opportunities to help you get there. Writing this affirmation in this way helps you remain focussed on your objectives, even if you get a setback.

Enjoy your success, you are living 'on purpose'.

By the way, you might like to know that great visionaries have been able to achieve so much and persist when everyone else has given up because they hold themselves fast to their vision. They were living a bolder life. Achievers focus on what they do want, not what they don't want. When they focus on their objectives they become like a heat-seeking missile, instead of scattering their energies and distracted with unproductive negative small thinking.

If what you've been doing so far hasn't produced any results, you may need to try something new. There will always be setbacks and disappointment for all of us.

If you've never had a burning desire to succeed at anything the exercise I've just taken you through will help you stay focussed and perhaps provide an inkling of what it should feel like to aim for fulfilment, success and happiness; with the will to aim for something stupendous.

Now, hands up those of you who have come this far and are thinking: "I still don't know what I really want!"

Relax, calm down, there's more to come. For some people carving out their own future and really nailing down what they are meant to do can take a long time. For others the goal that they may set themselves might appear totally out of their reach or seem unrealistic at the moment.

This is why this book delivers its message as a stepped process. All the tools which form the 7 Core Principles are there for a very good reason and help you take the right steps in the right order. It is during the process of organising yourself, re-shaping your life and eliminating useless stuff which creates the space ready to usher in new opportunities.

Some ideas and ambitions take a while to mature and like a good wine or a strong cheese you can't hurry perfection, or take any short-cuts. Half the fun is the journey to get there and the process and time taken to achieve your objective.

For instance, you may want to write a book but haven't a dedicated room in your house that you can turn into a study. Maybe you don't have a computer and don't know where the money for that will come from. Perhaps you've a home to run, four children and a full time job, but secretly would love to design clothes. If you want something badly enough, are prepared to do some work, make some sacrifices and to find a way to make it happen, everything in this book is here to help you achieve that.

You may start out with one plan (or no plan at all), but may end up doing something entirely different, purely because your mind has suddenly seen some options. You may have a vague fuzzy notion of what you want to achieve but turning that into something concrete may take a while. We've been so used to 'having it all now' that we may have forgotten that the journey to get what we want should be just as exciting and fulfilling as the results. Why? Because on that journey, you learn things, you meet people on the way, you overcome a challenge, and you excel yourself. Then you will take pride on your achievements, and by helping others, you take yourself personally and professionally to a much higher level.

Only after you've worked through the previous 6 Core Principles will you be better placed to know how to achieve your objective, because by then you will have removed virtually all the 'interference' blocking your path, which will in time will be replaced by a newer, super charged, more invigorated version of yourself.

Some people I know have, found themselves following new pathways after going through this process . Granted they did not have all the answers at the outset. However, they knew that instinctively it was the best choice for them and it felt right. It was only later on that they saw that every disappointment, every lesson, every person they've met had in some way been relevant to their ultimate purpose. They followed their instincts and it all worked out in the end.

Therefore if you trust your instincts, your subconscious mind (the RAS) will take you exactly where you want to go and will work on your behalf 24 hours a day to get you there. Keep watching out for clues, coincidences, opportunities, guides and prompts which let you know you are heading in the right direction. It's your feelings that will give you the clues to let you know if something is right or wrong for you.

The Celestine Prophecy states that you should only take action when your feeling is inviting and positive. Then the actions you take will be aligned with the Higher Will.

Case Study: Getting Out Of Your Own Way

Jessica had a complete mental block about starting her own business. She was spending a lot of time talking about it, but wasn't actually taking any action. She was lost in the detail, focussing on why she wasn't getting anything done.

I used an exercise to walk her through the logical levels I mentioned at the beginning of this book. This exercise is carried out a series of steps across the floor. As I literally walked her across the carpet, halfway through the exercise I could see that something was causing her to feel quite emotional. We continued and eventually reached the highest point on the logical levels at the point where I felt it was time to ask 'the question' which is usually reserved for the higher self.

The exercise prepares you to receive this question. Some people refer to the higher self as God, spirit, higher consciousness and within the context of the mastermind principle the Third Mind. This question is "Close your eyes and take as long as you like to connect with the best and highest thing you can imagine, that which is beyond anything you have been exploring, whether you think of that as God, your highest self, connection with others, or how it all connects with the big picture of your life. Now that you are connected, let me ask you: who are you in this area of your life?"

If you recall at the beginning of this book I talk about interference and 'getting out of your own way'. In our normal day-to-day lives we routinely struggle to get in touch with our higher self due to interference. This is basically because as I said earlier life gets in the way! So, we would normally struggle to answer this question.

Jessica thought for a moment but then she finally said, "I'm a mum". This revelation really shocked her and she wasn't really sure where this answer came from.

She'd had difficulty in acknowledging her role in this area, which paradoxically prevented her from moving on and making a start on her business. Her children were extremely important to her of course, but she'd always thought of herself as a career woman. She'd given up a good job in London to spend more time at home with her children but was having difficulty making the adjustment. Her identity was more closely aligned to being a career woman than as a stay-at-home mum, which created mixed feelings about her role.

She admitted to me that initially she didn't see the value in doing this exercise but her reaction to it really took her by surprise. Once she acknowledged and accepted that she was both a career woman and a mother she then went on to completely re-write her business plan, develop her brand and take a quantum leap forward with her business. For her the interference was the confusion around her identity. Once we'd cleared that up she was on her way.

ENERGY - ANOTHER SPORTING ANALOGY

Simon Barnes writes in 'The Times': *"Rugby is a game of violence. It is supposed to be. Both codes. It is a game of brutal physical confrontations: individual against individual, group against group. That is, if you like, the point. All the territorial ball games are mimic battles and rugby is the closest sport gets to the real thing. All the more reason, then, for it not to go over the edge.*

"Without violence, rugby is nothing. Would the streets of London have been lined for the winners of the Touch-Rugby

World Cup? I think not. But violence is not the whole of the game. Rugby is not 15-man or 13-man boxing. Violence is the setting, the context. Without violence there is no courage, without mayhem there is no grace, without pain there is no exalted relief in victory. Memo to all who run both codes of the game: rugby is a mimic war. When we want real war, we turn to the front of the newspaper."

I love watching rugby. I think it's one of the most exciting and exhilarating games there is. But, possibly not one I'd like to participate in myself. Each week rugby internationals experience the agony and the ecstasy of the game – but they accept that pain is part of the bargain because they are doing what they love. They put their body and soul on the line in every match and it's their passion for the game which overrides everything else. It's their purpose and almost their entire reason for being. However, consider this, if they didn't have rugby where do you think all that energy, fire and passion would go?

Energy has to move in one direction or another but for some people this energy is not always directed positively. This is why it's important to identify something that gives your life some purpose.

Ask yourself, where is all your energy being directed at the moment? Is it being put to good use or wasted on trifling and petty annoyances? Does it drive your success or is it putting the brakes on your progress? If it is stagnating or moving in the wrong direction, you are wasting a precious resource.

So how can you direct this energy positively?

THE POWER OF INTENTION

We are irresistibly drawn towards people with a can-do attitude and a high degree of certainty about them. They are solution focussed all the way, even when they don't know quite how they will achieve their objective. They put all their energy into their intention, make a decision and go for it, and then trust that their path will appear.

A tool to help you direct your energy is the power of Intention. You could call it the 'supercharge' button which helps you achieve a goal. That is why the phrase "be careful what you ask for, because you might just get it" rings true. But you have to know what you want. I have proved this over and over to myself.

THERE'S NO PLACE LIKE HOME

Let me explain. A few years ago I made the decision to move out of my flat and buy a house. At the time, the realistic possibility of buying a house on my salary was completely out of the question. I was living in a flat beneath the neighbour from hell. I recall sitting up in bed one night and affirming to myself: "I don't know how I'm going to achieve this but I'm going to get a house and I'll do everything I can to make it happen." I was desperate to feel safe, secure and contented in my own home and was completely fed up with the intrusion into my peaceful tranquillity that the noise created. You could say that I intentionally decided for myself the outcome that I wanted.

Four months later I bought my house and moved in. Something else took over and helped me to engineer an outcome that was in my favour.

Intention can get people moving and is a key component in achievement. However, some people doubt or don't believe its power. If you believe and trust in yourself then by intentionally resolving to do something you are actually saying: "This is who I am, and this is what I want and by the way – I intend to get it!" Even shouting your intention out to the universe is all that's required.

However a word of caution. Be mindful of what other people's intentions are, because they may mean well but go about things the wrong way. This can lead to misunderstandings, particularly if they don't articulate their intentions that well. Like the song goes, "I'm just a soul who's intentions are good, oh Lord please don't let me be misunderstood".

Intention doesn't necessarily work in every case, particularly if your plans are not aligned with your highest and best purpose. Then you may need to detach from the outcome if you suspect that things might not go quite the way you'd planned them to.

If you have a big ambition, a hope or desire (which is clean and legal of course) and need something to galvanise you into action, intentionally decide something today and make a resolution with yourself.

CERCA TROVA – SEEK AND YOU SHALL FIND

So, you've made your decision, you are intentionally going after something. What's next? How do you attract the people or find the way forward?

The best way is to utilise The Law of Attraction.

This is one of the key factors in bringing people and opportunities towards you instead of 'pushing the river' to engineer results that might feel slightly contrived and unsatisfying.

To illustrate my point let's consider a fascinating TV documentary about a painting by Leonardo Da Vinci called "The Battle of Anghiari". This is sometimes referred to as "The Lost Leonardo". It is believed to be hidden beneath Vasari's Fresco "The Battle of Marciano" in the Hall of Five Hundred in the Palazzo Vecchio, Florence.

Once considered the masterpiece beyond masterpieces, recovering it would be like discovering a new "Mona Lisa" or a new "Last Supper".

Now a hint to the whereabouts of "The Lost Leonardo" may have been painted on a tiny green flag in the gigantic 39-by-26-foot fresco as a clue to the location of the "Battle of Anghiari." On the flag are written the words Cerca Trova – translated this means "Seek And You Shall Find".

And that is my question to you. What is it that you are searching for and if you haven't found it yet - are you looking in the right place?

It may be career success, a pay rise, more clients, recognition, a promotion or just escape from the rat race. But whatever you want I have some little clues for you that may help you get closer to the answer which is, I believe, right under your nose.

Warning: If you are the sort of person who doesn't believe in coincidences or chance events or 'gut instinct', please look away now.

For the rest of you here are 11 'clues' to where the answer is hidden...

1. Ask for help from within – your subconscious. Trust your own judgement, for here resides the most phenomenal power available to you for free – but only if you believe!

2. This might sound a bit esoteric but deepening your spiritual connection and waiting for the answers sometimes works.

3. Act on any 'prompts' you receive – these could be throw-away comments from other people, something you hear on the radio, a song or a book that falls out of the bookshelf in the library.

4. Avoid negative influences, energy vampires and thought viruses given to you by others that could deter you from reaching your goal.

5. Write a task list but try writing some tasks for the Universe to help you with as well, for example: "Who can help me with this challenge?" or "What else do I need to know here?" Again wait for the answers.

6. Be open to receive and don't sabotage the results by being doubtful.

7. Be grateful for what comes your way.

8. Listen and be open to these answers – they come in surprising packages. Once you tap into the global consciousness you can watch as serendipity and coincidences start to happen all over the place.

9. Up your peer group. You may need to fire some people from your life who don't empathise or support you on your journey. Being around positive, affirming people lifts your spirit and sets the bar higher and could introduce you to the perfect person you need right now.

10. Read motivational material and stay away from doom and gloom merchants (don't read the daily newspapers!)

11. Be on purpose. Take action every day even when things don't appear to be manifesting for you. Stay hopeful. They will.

IS IT TIME FOR YOU TO TAKE MASSIVE ACTION?

Right at the start of this book is a quote by Napoleon Hill from his Book 'Think and Grow Rich'. He said of the Mastermind principle: *"The human mind is a form of energy, a part of it being spiritual in nature. When the minds of two people are coordinated in a spirit of harmony, the spiritual units of energy of each mind form an affinity, which constitutes the 'psychic' phase of the Master Mind."*

SET UP YOUR OWN MASTER MIND GROUP

Andrew Carnegie's Master Mind group consisted of a staff of approximately fifty men with whom he surrounded himself for the definite purpose of manufacturing and marketing steel. He attributed his entire fortune to the power he accumulated through this "Master Mind".

Your Master Mind group can meet once a week face to face or over the telephone/Skype to assign time for each person's challenge. Your combined minds will generate innovative solutions and inspirational ideas that your mind on it's own would never be able to achieve. Imagine that - 4 more brains or 8 more brains working on your behalf! Isn't that better than sitting in your office struggling alone on a problem thinking, "there isn't an answer". Trust me, there is always an answer. My sister Jules is ALWAYS reminding me of that fact.

A logical, linear approach does work, because here you are only working at a conscious level. As an example of a lateral approach Isaac Newton's discovery of the spectrum of light didn't take place when he was consciously looking for it. He was very curious and open to new ideas and concepts. One day he bought a prism at the Stourbridge Fair and spent an entire afternoon lying on the floor of his lab and watched as the sun shone through the prism. He was fascinated by the colours that were reflected on the wall, which led to his discovery of the spectrum of light.

Mostly all great inventions, ideas and solutions resulted from applying lateral thinking. It is the quality of your thinking that is the key here. When you join with other minds this thinking is amplified thus accelerating the flow of new ideas.

"No two minds ever came together without thereby creating a third, invisible intangible force, which may be linked to a third mind."
Napoleon Hill, Think and Grow Rich

LET'S TALK ABOUT MIND/BUBBLE MAPS

A practical exercise which can help you transfer what is in your head into a tangible 'something' or a concrete plan is Mind Mapping.

I use mind maps when I'm 'stuck' and just can't work out how to start a project or a challenge which is so overwhelming it causes me stress. This will work for all those practical down to earth people who like to 'see' things on paper and aren't that much struck on abstract thinking or visualisation.

According to Tony Buzan the originator of mind mapping, *"A Mind Map is a powerful graphic technique which provides a universal key to unlock the potential of the brain.*

"It harnesses the full range of cortical skills - word, image, number, logic, rhythm, colour and spatial awareness - in a single, uniquely powerful manner. In so doing, it gives you the freedom to roam the infinite expanses of your brain.

"The Mind Map can be applied to every aspect of life where improved learning and clearer thinking will enhance human performance."

Originated in the late 1960s mind maps are now used by millions of people around the world - from the very young to the very old - whenever they wish to use their minds more effectively.

It's useful to take yourself with a pad and pen to a quiet place or a coffee shop. Plug yourself into some music, switch off and allow your mind to drift. Don't censor your thoughts either. It's not about finding 'the right answer'. If you're a perfectionist this may be a challenge, so give yourself a break and please go with it. A mind map is there to explore all the options and identify possibilities, so put a gag on the inner critic or voice that says, "that will never happen". What is produced will form the basis of an action plan.

Mind maps help identify the 'what if' scenarios as well. Once you start it will be easy to put together a plan to collate all the relevant information. From there you can devise a way forward and execute your plan. It will open your mind to the possibilities that weren't there before. You might be interested to know that the concept for this book was initially developed through a mind map.

Give it a try. Visit Tony Buzan's website at *www.buzanworld.com* to find out more.

Case Study: How Do You Eat An Aeroplane?

Dee was looking for answers. She started her business in interior design after a long career working in the City of London for a large corporate firm. She was having problems connecting with her USP (Unique Selling Point).

"I can't quite pin down what it is that I'm offering, I'm completely confused and don't know where to start!"

Firstly, I encouraged her to do some mind mapping. I said that she wouldn't necessarily get the answer straight away but that this process was to evaluate and dig deep to discover what was special about her that she wasn't currently aware of.

So I set her some 'homework'.

Firstly she was to put on some motivational music, get several large pieces of paper or a dry-wipe board, lots of different coloured pens and look at the following three questions:

---

1. "What inspires me?"
2. "What have I done in my career that I'm really proud of?"
3. "What do other people tell me over and over that's different and unique about me?"

Then she was to mind-map whatever came into her mind but without censoring her answers.

I also asked her a question: "If I were to give you a cheque for £10,000 and paid you to do whatever you really wanted, what would that be?"

To help her complete this mind mapping process I encouraged her to utilise the following:

- Use a dry wipe board to make lists and prioritise.
- Find the right kind of support.
- Book meetings with key people.
- Do more research as a result of the information gathered.
- Plan her next steps and develop an action plan.
- Work her plan every day.

All this 'evidence' would then be put together to help her find the missing pieces of her puzzle so that she would know what her Unique Selling Point was. All these strategies chunked down a big question into smaller bite-sized morsels so that the problem didn't seem quite so overwhelming. Dee moved forward with a plan, using a process of analysis and elimination. This ultimately brought her closer to the answer to the question that vexed her.

So the answer to the question: "How do you eat an aeroplane?" Answer - one piece at a time.

INTRODUCING THE PPPPPPP PRINCIPLE:

So, you know what you want and you know where you're going. How do you execute your plan? Years ago a chap I knew who was in the army, shared a phrase his platoon used which was "Prior Preparation and Planning, Prevents P*ss Pot Performance".

I once worked in a large IT Development Department and one day the management had a meeting and decided that they wanted to restructure and reorganise the department, consisting of 100 programmers, analysts and project managers. They also had to incorporate six more desks into the office which was almost full to capacity already. Now in normal circumstances you would think this was relatively straightforward, but there was another challenge. We had to execute this operation with no interruption to the service the department provided to the rest of the business, plus relocate some essential equipment (a large switch cabinet and a few smaller servers) elsewhere.

I was given the responsibility for this and had six weeks to complete the task. I therefore had to undertake the most meticulous planning, as any mistake could prove disastrous to the business as a whole. My first job was to gain cooperation from everyone and believe me not everyone wanted to move (some people are really territorial when it comes to their workstation!)

Some of the programmers had their own servers and didn't want them taken away from them and consequently were very territorial about them. We had Oracle Developers, Java Developers, Business Analysts, Programme Testers, Project Managers, all working on numerous projects; and of course I had to make sure that the IT Technical Support team were available to move all the screens, keyboards and phones and transfer all the data and telephony and achieve this over a weekend.

It was a mammoth undertaking. Every single detail had to be taken care of – it was like working on a giant Rubik's cube against the clock.

When the day finally arrived we started at 12.00 midday on Friday. I sent one team out to lunch while we moved their desks and rotated this throughout the rest of the afternoon, continuing into Saturday and Sunday. By Monday morning it was business as usual and the only problem we encountered was one broken keyboard.

"You look them straight in the eye and say, 'Don't tell me it's impossible until after I've already done it'."
Pam Lontos, Head of PR/PR Public Relations

ACTION POINTS - VISION

- Start to connect your vision
- Decide to intentionally focus on what you want
- Mind map and explore some options
- Cultivate a can-do success mindset
- Develop an action plan
- Work your plan

Vision Power Question
If you could wave a magic wand and wake up tomorrow with everything exactly how you wanted it what would you see?

Tom had never, ever considered the possibility of waking up every morning feeling connected to his purpose and up until now he'd never thought that trees were his connection with his higher calling as a human being. He'd been running around making about as much impact as a snail. He'd never had the wherewithal to convert his passion for garden design and the wide open spaces into a plan. But now he'd 'woken up' his whole thinking started to shift.

Someone sitting opposite him was reading the paper and a small article caught Tom's eye: 'From Futures Trader to Tree Surgeon'. He was trying desperately to read the small print without drawing attention to himself. He was hoping they'd leave the paper behind when they left. Tom was inspired to get started straight away to find out how other people were changing their lives and how they were achieving this.

Louisa's train had been delayed and had crawled to the last three stops, which gave her plenty of time to eat up every last word in the book. When she arrived at her stop Louisa had also turned a corner. She was more enlightened. Whereas before she 'didn't know what she didn't know', now she realised that a lot of what had happened to her was because of how she felt about herself. If she changed that then surely other people would change towards her as the same time?

As she walked up the high street she passed by the shoe shop. There in the window were the most exquisite pair of shimmering red shoes. The old Louisa would never own anything like these. She needed to find a way to let the leader in her emerge, and one way would be to dress, talk and behave like the person she felt was lurking inside. All that energy and determination had to translate off the hockey pitch as well as on it. Therefore, she needed to aim higher, and if she wasn't being supported in her quest, she must find the right place where she would be.

She stared at the shoes and what they represented. If other people sensed greatness, her power and her potential and didn't like it, it was their problem, not hers any longer. Would the team Captain of the hockey team wear those? "You try and stop me!"

If Dan was honest he'd struggled with his definition of 'success'. Yes money was very important to him but focussing on this to exclusion of everything else had rendered success empty and meaningless. To get 'success' he'd turned himself into an exhausted, frazzled and moody so-and-so. He'd been chasing success, but now he'd got there it didn't really mean anything. If he was totally honest with himself he'd had more fun sitting in the pub all afternoon reading this book than he'd had in a long time.

He realised that his whole working life was geared around booking the next holiday and constantly rewarding himself because his day-to-day existence was so stressful. All it had brought him was a stomach ulcer. He knew it was time to turn the corner and live his life in a new way, and look for happiness and fulfilment rather than being hooked on all the trappings of success. What good was a plasma TV if he was six feet under? He got up to leave and remembered the little dog who had attached itself to his foot. Before he knew it he'd agreed to take the dog home with him. His daughter Sophie would love that, but his wife would probably go berserk.

His wife called him. "Yes I know I've been in the pub for 6 hours. And no I'm not drunk (this time). Put the kettle on, I've got something to tell you. Err and I'm bringing a friend home with me."

He gathered up his coat and the little Schnauzer, and walked to his car.

"Oh Joy, Rapture! I've got a brain!"
The Scarecrow, the Wizard of Oz

For those that know who they are, what they want and where they're going, the rewards are higher and the world really is their oyster.

The Emerald City...

So, my friends, we've finally reached the end of this book.

This book won't give you the answer to everything, it's not The Holy Grail, but at the very least it's got you thinking, hasn't it? Without taking action none of the material in this book is of any value. So it's now up to you.

PUTTING IT ALL TOGETHER

Is there is something special you'd like to work on?

- Get a promotion.
- Be taken more seriously in meetings.
- Feel more confident in your role.
- Implement a grand plan.
- Become a better leader.
- Become a beacon to motivate and inspire others.
- Develop a new business idea.
- Change career direction entirely.
- Improve your relationships.

Please use the Personal Workshop Planning Activities to draw up your own action plan to take yourself forward. These can be found in the Appendix

"In my films I celebrate the imagination as a tool of great creations... I dream for a living. Once a month, the sky falls on my head, I come to, and I see another movie I want to make. Sometimes I think I've got ball bearings for brains; these ideas are slipping and sliding across each other all the time. My problem is that my imagination won't turn off. I wake up so excited, I can't eat breakfast. I've never run out of energy."
Stephen Spielberg, American Film Director, Screen Writer and Producer

Appendix

PERSONAL WORKSHOP PLANNING ACTIVITY

Principle 1 - Environment: What changes will you make this week, e.g. time management, lifestyle or health?

```
┌──────────────────────────────────────────────┐
│                                                │
│                                                │
│                                                │
│                                                │
└──────────────────────────────────────────────┘
```

Principle 2 – Capabilities: What do you need to evaluate here? e.g. are there any skills gaps that need filling, or what transferable skills do you possess that need dusting off?

```
┌──────────────────────────────────────────────┐
│                                                │
│                                                │
│                                                │
└──────────────────────────────────────────────┘
```

Principle 3 – Attitude: Is there anything you need to change or needs some improvement?

```
┌──────────────────────────────────────────────┐
│                                                │
│                                                │
│                                                │
└──────────────────────────────────────────────┘
```

Principle 4 – Packaging: What aspects of your image need modifying? Do you talk with conviction?

Principle 5 – Beliefs: What beliefs are getting in the way of your success? What new beliefs do you need to bring forth in order for you to design your own future?

Principle 6 - Values: Write down what's important to you about your life and career, what's missing and what have you compromised on for far too long?

Principle 7 – Vision: Go there first – write down your perfect day and if you had everything how you wanted it, what would that look, sound and feel like?

Now, write down your goals and the tasks and activities that you will undertake over the next 90 days.

90 DAY PERSONAL ACTION PLAN

Use this 90 Day Action Plan. Set yourself some activities which fall into 30, 60 or 90 day slots.

Task	Difficulty			Timescales			Activity
	E	M	D	30	60	90	
Time Management/ Health/Lifestyle							
Capabilities/Skills							
Attitude							
Image/Communication/ Body Language							
Beliefs/Assumptions							
Values/Intention							
Vision/Planning/Action							

FURTHER READING

Persuasion Engineering, Bandler, R & La Valle, J, Meta Publishing

The Aladdin Factor, Canfield, J & Victor Hanson, M, Berkley Inspiration

Presenting Magically, James, T & Shepherd, D, Crown House

The Sedona Method, Howskin, D, Sedona Press

I Can Make You Rich, McKenna, P, Bantam Press

From Acorns, How to Build Your Brilliant Business from Scratch, Woods, C, Pearson, Prentice Hall Business

The Beermat Entrepreneur, Southern, M & West, C, Pearson, Prentice Hall Business

A Friend in Every City, Power, P & Power, T & Coote, A, Ecademy Press

Rich Dad Poor Dad, Kiyosaki, RT, Warner Bros Books With Sharon Lechter

You Inc., Hedges, B, Inti Publishing

Coach Yourself to Success, Miedaner, T, Contemporary Books

The Business Coaching Handbook, Martin, C, Crown House

Dig Your Well Before You're Thirsty, Mackay, H, Currency Press

Feel the Fear and Do It Anyway, Jeffers, S, Arrow

The E-Myth Revisited, Gerber, M, Harper Business

What They Don't Teach You at Harvard Business School, McCormack, MH, Fontana/Collins

Excuse Me, Your Life is Waiting, Grabhorn, L, Hodder Mobius

How I Made It, Bridge, R, The Sunday Times

Emotional Intelligence, Goleman, D, Bloomsbury Paperbacks

The Work We Were Born To Do, Williams, N, Element

The Luck Factor, Wiseman, R, Random House

A Message to Garcia & Other Essays, Hubbard, E, Sun Publishing

They F**** You Up: How to Survive Family Life, James, O, Bloomsbury

The 7 Habits of Highly Effective People, Covey, SR, Simon & Schuster Ltd

The Celestine Prophecy, Redfield, J & Adrienne, C, Bantam Books

The New Conceptual Selling, Miller, RB, & Heiman, SE, with Tuleja, T, Business Plus

Who Moved My Cheese?, Johnson, S, Vermillion

…And Death Came Third, Lopata, A & Roper, P, Lean Marketing Press

NLP The New Technology Of Achievement, Andreas, S, & Faulkner, C Nicholas Brealey Publishing Ltd

Synchro Destiny, Chopra, D, Random House

Who Do You Think, You Are Anyway? Rohm, RA, & Carey, EC, Personality Insights

French Women Don't Get Fat, Guiliano, M, Chatto & Windus

Secrets of the Millionaire Mind, Eker, TH, Piatkus

Signposts – The Universe Is Whispering to You, Linn, D, Rider

Spiritual Marketing, Vitale, J, 1st Books Library

The Hidden Messages in Water, Emoto, M, Atria Books

Time Management for Dummies, Evans, C, John Wiley & Sons

Coachville, *www.coachville.com*

Daniel Goleman, *www.danielgoleman.info/blog*

Robert Dilts, *www.nlpu.com*

The Image Practice, *www.theimagepractice.co.uk*

John Levine's Alpha Music, *www.silenceofmusic.com*

45 Steps You Absolutely Have To Take To Succeed After Redundancy, *www.resolutioncoaching.co.uk*

Emotional Freedom Technique, *www.emofree.com*

National Debtline, *www.nationaldebtline.org.uk*

Consumer Credit Counselling Service (UK) 0800 1381111

The Pensions Advisory Service (UK) 0845 601 2923

Financial Services Authority, *www.moneymadeclear.fsa.gov.uk*

One2Three Commercial Ltd (Specialists in Personal Debt), *www.One2threecommercial.co.uk*

Forever Living, *www.aloeveraforever.ws* / *www.foreverliving.com*

ACKNOWLEDGEMENTS

The "Belief Assessment Sheet" is an extract from "Sleight of Mouth" (Published by Met Publications) and reproduced with kind permission of the author Robert Dilts.

The extract taken from "Emotional Intelligence" (Published by Bloomsbury Paperbacks) is reproduced with kind permission of the author Daniel Goleman.

Extract from "Finding your Irresistible Voice Audio Series" kind permission of Jonathan Altfeld *www.altfeld.com/mastery/index.html*

Extracts from "Is A Tidy Desk The Sign Of A Sick Mind" reproduced with kind permission of www.sedona.com

"In everyone's life, at some time, our inner fire goes out. It is then burst into flame by an encounter with another human being. We should all be thankful for those people who rekindle the inner spirit."

Albert Schweitzer, Alsation Theologian, Musician and Philosopher

About the Author

Wendy began her career as a Girl Friday in TV and Radio Advertising in the West End of London when she was 19. She has 25 years experience as a PA in the public and private sector supporting executives at all levels. Wendy's coaching skills were forged at the tender age of 10 whilst working for her dad in London during the summer holidays. Being in the 'eye of the storm' Wendy and her four sisters were given a unique insight into the highs and lows of running a business, and the impact this had on her father and the family as a whole. Her background, training and expertise has given her great insight into what makes a professional tick. Her capacity to communicate and connect with people at all levels is truly unique.

Wendy qualified as a Personal Coach with The Coaching Academy in 2004 and is a Licensed Practitioner of Neuro-Linguistic Programming (NLP), having undertaken some of her training with both Paul McKenna and Richard Bandler. Wendy is a Qualified Level II Practitioner in Emotional Freedom Technique (EFT). Wendy is also a trained career mentor and has a background in holistic therapies. Wendy has introduced scores of people to coaching and has helped small business owners, entrepreneurs and executives 'get out of their own way' and forge successful careers whilst still having a life.

Wendy is the author of '45 Steps You Absolutely Have To Take To Succeed After Redundancy', 'What Planet Are

You On? DISC The Secrets of the Cosmos and You' and 'The Secrets of Champions' and has been quoted in Pass Magazine and Prima.

She is a member of the International Coaching Federation.

Discover Who You Are, What You Want and Where You're Going at *www.resolutioncoaching.co.uk*

Good Question!

the art of asking questions to bring about positive change

Judy Barber

Richard Wilkins, Mark Forster, Coen de Groot, David Ure, Deepak Lodhia, Ewemade Orobator, David Hyner, Gary Outrageous, Julie French, Richard Tod, Tessa Lovemore, George Metcalfe, Martin Haworth, Steve Halls, Gérard Jakimavicius, Joe Armstrong, Wendy Sullivan, Sanjay Shah, Tony Burgess, Jamie Smart, Debbie Jenkins, Gerard O'Donovan, Jesvir Mahil, Jean Houston, Chris Howe, Lisa Wynn, Babu Shah, Aboodi Shabi, Lourdes Callen

www.bookshaker.com

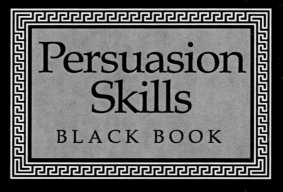

Persuasion Skills

BLACK BOOK

*Practical NLP Language Patterns for
Getting The Response You Want*

Rintu Basu

FREE INSIDE
'Black Book'
Persuasion
Training
E-course

www.bookshaker.com

Printed in the United Kingdom by
Lightning Source UK Ltd., Milton Keynes
139221UK00001B/10/P